AEROFILMS GUIDE

FOOTBALL

GROUNDS

AEROFILMS GUIDE

THIRD REVISED EDITION

FOOTBALL
GROUNDS

Edited by Dave Twydell

DIAL HOUSE

CONTENTS

Page 1: One of the most dramatic of the second-generation grounds completed in recent years is the Alfred McAlpine Stadium in Huddersfield, which opened at the start of the 1994/95 season.

Page 3: Jack Walker's millions have not just gone in the building of an impressive squad at Blackburn Rovers, but also in helping to turn Ewood Park into a ground fit for Champions.

First published in 1993
Reprinted 1993 (Twice)
Second edition 1994
Third edition 1995

ISBN 0 7110 2376 X

Published by Dial House

an imprint of Ian Allan Ltd, Terminal House, Station Approach, Shepperton, Surrey KT15 1HY

Printed by Ian Allan Printing Ltd, Coombelands House, Addlestone, Weybridge, Surrey KT15 1HY

Aerial photography ©

Aerofilms

Hunting Aerofilms Limited have been specialists in aerial photography since 1919. Their library of aerial photographs, both new and old, is in excess of 1.5 million images. Aerofilms undertake to commission oblique and vertical survey aerial photography which is processed and printed in their specialised photographic laboratory. Digital photomaps are prepared using precision scanners. The Company has been a subsidiary of Hunting plc since 1936.

Free photostatic proofs are available on request for any site held within the collection and price lists will be forwarded detailing the sizes of photographic enlargement available without obigation to purchase.

Text © Ian Allan Ltd 1993, 1994, 1995
Football action photography © Empics
Photographs of Wembley reproduced by kind permission of Wembley plc

Editor's Note

The second edition of the *Aerofilms Guide: Football Grounds* was again very well received especially since this included views of all the Scottish League clubs. The fact that most of the Scottish grounds have only been given coverage by way of an oblique aerial photograph is not intended to belittle these clubs, but pure economic considerations have necessitated the limitation of number of pages in this book. Changes still continue to the Grounds, including those of Scotland, and the time lapse between the photography (ideally taken during the season to ensure pitch markings, etc.) and the publication of this book inevitably leads to later additional changes to some grounds. Apart from the logistic difficulties in tracking down all previous or proposed changes, it also has to be appreciated that such improvements are sometimes undertaken at short notice, or indeed without any advanced notification. All the Grounds that were known to have visually changed since the 1993/94 season were photographed during the following season, and building work can often be seen in some of the pictures. In some cases this work may have been completed after this book went to the printers and in other cases we show grounds complete and intact where work will have subsequently begun. Additionally a number of previously used vertical views have been repeated for convenience, despite new oblique views which have been included. We will, of course, continue to update the coverage as fully as possible in future editions of this book. As before we have made every effort to ensure that all the information given in the entries is accurate and complete, but changes being made to the grounds, a lack of response from some clubs, and other factors beyond the publisher's control may introduce errors for which the publisher can admit no consequential responsibility.

We would like to thank the majority of clubs who took the time and trouble to reply to our requests for information and updates. We would also like to thank the Empics photo agency of Nottingham who supplied the football action pictures of each club which are also featured in this book, plus a special acknowledgement to Michael Matthews and Fay Twydell for their assistance. We also gratefully acknowledge the help provided by various members of the *Scottish '38' Club* (formed for those interested especially in visiting Scottish League grounds); for details send a SAE to Mark Byatt, 6, Greenfields Close, Loughton, Essex.

About the Author

Dave Twydell has, for many years, been a Brentford FC supporter and also follows non-League football. His first book *Defunct FC* (self-published) in 1986 led to his growing interest in the history of the game and the Football Grounds themselves. Six more books and several booklets followed, including *"Grounds For A Change"* (the histories of the former Grounds of the Football League clubs). Formerly a Chartered Structural Engineer, redundancy in 1991 led to the full-time publishing of football books - generally of an historic nature - under the 'Yore Publications' banner, with the principal assistance of wife (Fay), and married daughter (Kara). Dave is also a partner in Trans Video Productions, who have included several football videos, notably *English Football Grounds — From Newcastle to Wembley*, for Ian Allan SBS Videos.

5

WEMBLEY

Wembley Stadium, Wembley HA9 0DW

Tel No: 0181-902 8833
Advance Tickets Tel No: 0181-900 1234
Brief History: Inaugurated for F.A. Cup Final of 1923, venue for many major national and international matches including World Cup Final of 1966. Also used for major occasions in other sports and as venues for rock concerts and other entertainments.

(Total) Current Capacity: 79,000 (all seated)
Nearest Railway Station: Wembley Complex (BR), Wembley Central (BR & Tube), Wembley Park (tube)
Parking (Car): Limited parking at ground and nearby
Parking (Coach/Bus): As advised by police
Police Force: Metropolitan

ARSENAL

Arsenal Stadium, Avenell Road, Highbury, London, N5 1BU

Tel No: 0171 226 0304
Advance Tickets Tel No: 0171 359 0131
League: F.A. Premier
Brief History: Founded 1886 as Royal Arsenal, changed to Woolwich Arsenal in 1891, and Arsenal in 1914. Former grounds: Plumstead Common, Sportsman Ground, Manor Ground (twice), moved to Arsenal Stadium (Highbury) in 1913. Record attendance 73,295
(Total) Current Capacity: 38,000 (all seated)

Club Colours: Red shirts with white sleeves, white shorts
Nearest Railway Station: Drayton Park & Finsbury Park. Arsenal (tube)
Parking (Car): Street Parking
Parking (Coach/Bus): Drayton Park
Police Force and Tel No: Metropolitan (0171 263 9090)
Disabled Visitors' Facilities
    Wheelchairs: Lower tier East Stand (few)
    Blind: Commentary available

KEY

C Club Offices
E Entrance(s) for visiting supporters

↑ North direction (approx)

❶ Avenell Road
❷ Highbury Hill
❸ Gillespie Road
❹ To Drayton Park BR Station (¼ mile)
❺ Arsenal Tube Station
❻ Clock End

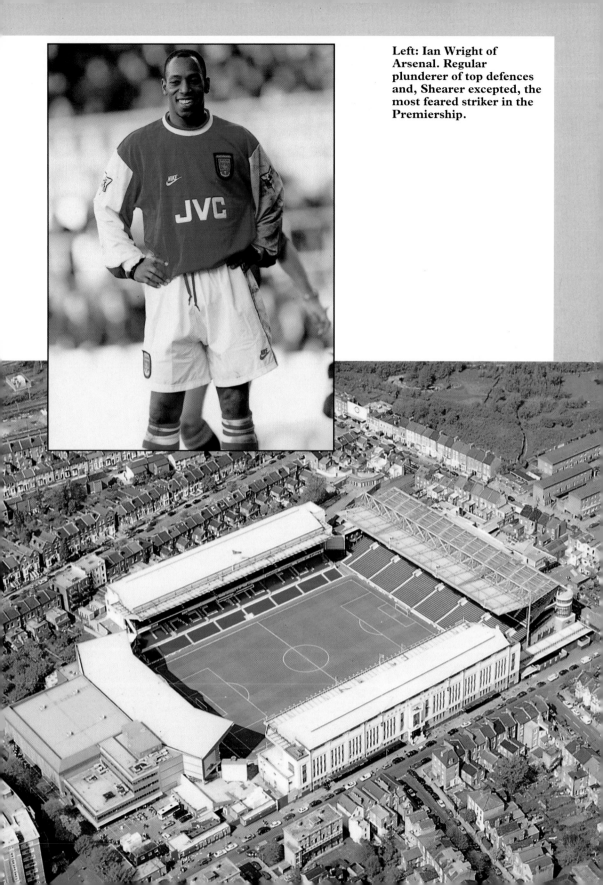

Left: Ian Wright of Arsenal. Regular plunderer of top defences and, Shearer excepted, the most feared striker in the Premiership.

ASTON VILLA

Villa Park, Trinity Road, Birmingham, B6 6HE

Tel No: 0121 327 2299
Advance Tickets Tel No: 0121 327 5353
Credit Card Sales: 0121 327 7373
League: F.A. Premier
Brief History: Founded in 1874. Founder Members Football League (1888). Former Grounds: Aston Park and Lower Aston Grounds & Perry Barr, moved to Villa Park (a development of the Lower Aston Grounds) in 1897. Record attendance 76,588
(Total) Current capacity: 40,100 (all seated)
Visiting Supporters' Allocation: Approx. 4,600 (all seated) in the Witton End 'R' block and Doug Ellis Stand lower 'Q' block.
Club Colours: Claret with blue stripe shirts, white shorts.

Nearest Railway Station: Witton
Parking (Car): Asda car park, Aston Hall Road
Parking (Coach/Bus): Asda car park, Aston Hall Road (special coach park for visiting supporters situated in Witton Lane).
Police Force and Tel No: West Midlands (021) 322 6010
Disabled Visitors' Facilities
　Wheelchairs: Trinity Road Stand section
　Blind: Commentary by arrangement

KEY
- **C** Club Offices
- **S** Club Shop
- **E** Entrance(s) for visiting supporters
- **R** Refreshment bars for visiting supporters
- **T** Toilets for visiting supporters

↑ North direction (approx)

❶ B4137 Witton Lane
❷ B4140 Witton Road
❸ Trinity Road
❹ A4040 Aston Lane to A34 Walsall Road
❺ To Aston Expressway & M6
❻ Holte End
❼ Visitors' Car Park

Left: Former Anfield favourite Steve Staunton in full flight for Villa last September. He also continues to earn International recognition for the Republic of Ireland.

BARNET

Underhill Stadium, Barnet Lane, Barnet, Herts, EN5 2BE

Tel No: 0181 441 6932
Advance Tickets Tel No: 0181 449 4173
Credit Card Bookings: 0181 441 1677
League: 3rd Division
Brief History: Founded 1888 as Barnet Alston. Changed name to Barnet (1919). Former grounds: Queens Road & Totteridge Lane. Promoted to Football League 1991. Record attendance 11,026.
(Total) Current capacity: Approx. 4,000 (approx 1,100 seated)
Visiting Supporters' Allocation: Approx. 900 (50% seated)
Club Colours: Amber & Black striped shirts, black shorts.

Nearest Railway Station: New Barnet (High Barnet - Tube)
Parking (Car): Street Parking & High Barnet Station
Parking (Coach/Bus): As directed by Police
Police Force and Tel No: Metropolitan (0181) 200 2212
Disabled Visitors' Facilities
  Wheelchairs: Barnet Lane (Social Club end - few spaces)
  Blind: No special facility
Anticipated Development(s): Temporary seated South Stand for 1995/96 season.

KEY
- **C** Club Offices
- **S** Club Shop
- **E** Entrance(s) for visiting supporters
- **R** Refreshment bars for visiting supporters
- **T** Toilets for visiting supporters

↑ North direction (approx)

❶ Barnet Lane
❷ Westcombe Drive
❸ A1000 Barnet Hill
❹ New Barnet BR Station (1 mile)
❺ To High Barnet Tube Station, M1 & M25

Left: Bees' Micky Tomlinson holds off the attentions of a Mansfield defender during this April 1995 encounter.

13

BARNSLEY

Oakwell Ground, Grove Street, Barnsley, S71 1ET

Tel No: 01226 295353
Advance Tickets Tel No: 01226 295353
League: 1st Division
Brief History: Founded 1887 as Barnsley St Peter's, changed name to Barnsley in 1897. Former Ground: Doncaster Road, Worsboro Bridge until 1888. Record attendance 40,255.
(Total) Current capacity: 19,050 (all seated)
Visiting Supporters' Allocation: 4,327 (seating in North Stand, plus uncovered seating behind goal)
Club Colours: Red shirts, white shorts

Nearest Railway Station: Barnsley Exchange
Parking (Car): Queen's Ground car park
Parking (Coach/Bus): Queen's Ground car park
Police Force and Tel No: South Yorkshire (01226) 206161
Disabled Visitors' Facilities
  Wheelchairs: Purpose Built Disabled Stand
  Blind: Commentary available
Anticipated Development(s): New all-seater Stand (capacity 4,500) at West End for completion August 1995.

KEY

C Club Offices
S Club Shop
E Entrance(s) for visiting supporters
R Refreshment bars for visiting supporters
T Toilets for visiting supporters

↑ North direction (approx)

❶ A628 Pontefract Road
❷ To Barnsley Exchange BR station and M1 Junction 37 (two miles)
❸ Queen's Ground Car Park

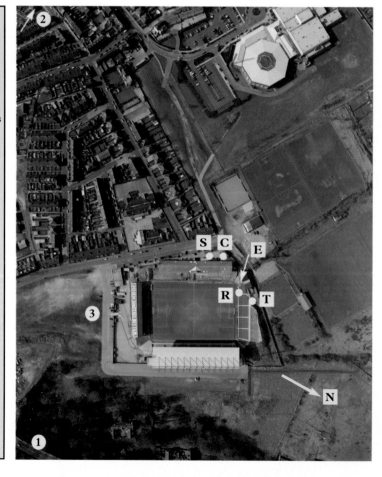

Right: Barnsley's Brendall O'Connell shields his eyes from the sun in an October 1994 Division One encounter at Oakwell.

BIRMINGHAM CITY

St Andrew's, St. Andrew's Street, Birmingham, B9 4NH

Tel No: 0121 772 0101
Advance Tickets Tel No: 0121 766 5743
Advance Tickets Kop Ticket Office: 0121 753 3408
League: 1st Division
Brief History: Founded 1875, as Small Heath Alliance. Changed to Small Heath in 1888, Birmingham in 1905, Birmingham City in 1945. Former Grounds: Arthur Street, Ladypool Road, Muntz Street, moved to St Andrew's in 1906. Record attendance 68,844.
(Total) Current Capacity: 25,000

Visiting Supporters' Allocation: 4,000
Club Colours: Blue shirts, Blue shorts
Nearest Railway Station: Birmingham New Street
Parking (Car): Street parking
Parking (Coach/Bus): Coventry Road
Police Force and Tel No: West Midlands (0121 772 1169)
Disabled Visitors' Facilities
Wheelchairs: Remploy stand (St Andrew's Street), advanced notice required.
Blind: No special facilities.

KEY

C Club Offices
S Club Shop
E Entrance(s) for visiting supporters
R Refreshment bars for visiting supporters
T Toilets for visiting supporters

↑ North direction (approx)

❶ Car Park
❷ B4128 Cattell Road
❸ Tilton Road
❹ Garrison Lane
❺ To A4540 & A38 (M)
❻ To City Centre and New Street BR Station (1½ miles)

Right: Ricky Otto in familiar pose on the Blues' wing. This tricky winger contributed in a large way to City's successful push for promotion to Division One.

BLACKBURN ROVERS

Ewood Park, Blackburn, Lancashire, BB2 4JF

Tel No: 01254 698888
Advance Tickets Tel No: 01254 698888
(696767 Credit card line)
League: F.A. Premier
Brief History: Founded 1875. Former Grounds:
Oozebooth, Pleasington Cricket Ground,
Alexandra Meadows. Moved to Ewood Park in
1890. Founder members of Football League
(1888). Record attendance 61,783.
(Total) Current Capacity: 31,146 (all seated)

Club Colours: Blue & white halved shirts, white
shorts
Nearest Railway Station: Blackburn
Parking (Car): Street parking
Parking (Coach/Bus): As directed by Police
Police Force and Tel No: Lancashire (01254
51212)
Disabled Visitors' Facilities
Wheelchairs : All sides of the ground
Blind: Commentary available.

KEY
C Club Offices
S Club Shop
E Entrance(s) for visiting
supporters
R Refreshment bars for visiting
supporters
T Toilets for visiting supporters

↑ North direction (approx)

❶ A666 Bolton Road
❷ Kidder Street
❸ Nuttall Street
❹ Town Centre & Blackburn
Central BR Station (1½
miles)
❺ To Darwen and Bolton
❻ Car parking area for 500 cars
❼ Car Parks
❽ Top O'Croft Road

Left: Perhaps, above all others, the man responsible for bringing the Title to Ewood Park – Colin Hendry, the rock at the centre of the Rovers' defence.

BLACKPOOL

Bloomfield Road, Blackpool, Lancashire, FY1 6JJ

Tel No: 01253 404331
Advance Tickets Tel No: 01253 404331
League: 2nd Division
Brief History: Founded 1887, merged with 'South Shore' (1899). Former grounds: Raikes Hall (twice) and Athletic Grounds, Stanley Park. South Shore played at Cow Cap Lane, moved to Bloomfield Road in 1899. Record attendance 38,098
(Total) Current Capacity: 9,654 (2,987 seated)
Visiting Supporters' Allocation: 2,300 min.(none seated)
Club Colours: Tangerine shirts, white shorts

Nearest Railway Station: Blackpool South
Parking (Car): At Ground & street parking (also behind West Stand - from M55)
Parking (Coach/Bus): Mecca car park (behind North End, (also behind West Stand - from M55)
Police Force and Tel No: Lancashire (01253 293933)
Disabled Visitors' Facilities
  Wheelchairs: By players entrance
  Blind: Commentary available
Anticipated Development(s): Plans for new ground/complex in same area anticipated to start 1996.

KEY
- **C** Club Offices
- **E** Entrance(s) for visiting supporters
- **S** Club Shop
- **R** Refreshment bars for visiting supporters
- **T** Toilets for visiting supporters

↑ North direction (approx)

- ❶ Car Parks
- ❷ To Blackpool South BR Station (1/2 mile) and M55 Junction 4
- ❸ Bloomfield Drive
- ❹ Central Drive
- ❺ Henry Street
- ❻ Blackpool Greyhound Stadium
- ❼ Blackpool Tower

Left: Blackpool's Chris Beech seems to be contemplating what might have been in a topsy turvy season for this once famous club.

BOLTON WANDERERS

Burnden Park, Manchester Road, Bolton, BL3 2QR

Tel No: 01204 389200
Advance Tickets Tel No: 01204 521101
League: FA Premier
Brief History: Founded 1874 as Christ Church until 1877. Former Grounds: Several Fields, moved to Pikes Lane in 1880, moved to Burnden Park in 1895. Founder-members of Football League (1888). Record attendance 69,912.
(Total) Current Capacity: 20,800 (7,400 seated)
Visiting Supporters' Allocation: 3,120 (standing only)
Club Colours: White shirts, blue shorts

Nearest Railway Station: Bolton Trinity Street
Parking (Car): Rosehill car park, Manchester Road
Parking (Coach/Bus): Rosehill car park, Manchester Road
Police Force and Tel No: Greater Manchester (01204 522466)
Disabled Visitors' Facilities
　Wheelchairs: Manchester Road (few)
　Blind: No special facility
Anticipated Development(s): By August 1996 the ground will be all seated, or relocation to a new ground will be in progress.

KEY
E Entrance(s) for visiting supporters
R Refreshment bars for visiting supporters
T Toilets for visiting supporters

↑ North direction (approx)

❶ Car Parks
❷ B6536 Manchester Road
❸ A666 St Peter's Way
❹ Bolton Trinity Street BR Station (1/2 mile)
❺ To M61 Junction 3 (3 miles)
❻ Supermarket

Left: Alan Stubbs has been likened to Alan Hansen at the heart of the Bolton defence and his calm, assured performances culminated in a successful promotion campaign via the Play-Offs.

A.F.C. BOURNEMOUTH

Dean Court, Bournemouth, Dorset BH7 7AF

Tel No: 01202 395381
Advance Tickets Tel No: 01202 395381
League: 2nd Division
Brief History: Founded 1890 as Boscombe St. John's, changed to Boscombe (1899), Bournemouth & Boscombe Athletic (1923) and A.F.C. Bournemouth (1971). Former grounds: Kings Park (twice) and Castlemain Road, Pokesdown. Moved to Dean Court in 1910. Record attendance 28,799.
(Total) Current Capacity: 11,880 (3,130 seated)
Visiting Supporters' Allocation: 2,190 (190 Seated Family Stand only).

Club Colours: Red with white `V' shirts, black with white piping shorts.
Nearest Railway Station: Bournemouth
Parking (Car): Large car park adjacent ground
Parking (Coach/Bus): Large car park adjacent ground
Police Force and Tel No: Dorset (01202) 552099
Disabled Visitors' Facilities
  Wheelchairs: South Stand (prior arrangement)
  Blind: No special facility

KEY
C Club Offices
S Club Shop
E Entrance(s) for visiting supporters
R Refreshment bars for visiting supporters
T Toilets for visiting supporters

⬆ North direction (approx)

❶ Car Park
❷ A338 Wessex Way
❸ To Bournemouth BR Station (1½ miles)
❹ To A31 & M27

Right: After a long career which has included spells at Manchester City and Barnsley, the much-travelled Mel Machin is now manager at Dean Court.

BRADFORD CITY

Valley Parade, Bradford, BD8 7DY

Tel No: 01274 306062
Advance Tickets Tel No: 01274 306062
League: 2nd Division
Brief History: Founded 1903 (formerly Manningham Northern Union Rugby Club founded in 1876). Continued use of Valley Parade, joined 2nd Division on re-formation. Record attendance 39,146.
(Total) Current Capacity: 14,810 (6,500 seated)
Club Colours: Claret & amber shirts, claret shorts

Nearest Railway Station: Bradford Forster Square

Parking (Car): Street parking and car parks

Parking (Coach/Bus): As directed by Police

Police Force and Tel No: West Yorkshire (01274 723422)

Disabled Visitors' Facilities
  Wheelchairs: N & P Stand
  Blind: No special facility

KEY

C Club Offices
E Entrance(s) for visiting supporters

↑ North direction (approx)

❶ Midland Road
❷ Valley Parade
❸ A650 Manningham Lane
❹ To City Centre, Forster Square and Interchange BR Stations M606 &M62
❺ To Keighley
❻ Car Parks

26

Right: City threatened the upper reaches of Division Two for the early months of last year, and much travelled Carl Shutt was one of the reasons for such a promising start.

BRENTFORD

Griffin Park, Braemar Road, Brentford, Middlesex, TW8 0NT

Tel No: 0181 847 2511
Advance Tickets Tel No: 0181 847 2511
League: 2nd Division
Brief History: Founded 1889. Former Grounds: Clifden House Ground, Benn's Field (Little Ealing), Shotters Field, Cross Roads, Boston Park Cricket Ground, moved to Griffin Park in 1904. Founder-members Third Division (1920). Record attendance 39,626.
(Total) Current Capacity: 13,870 (4,000 seated)
Visiting Supporters' Allocation: 2,263 (636 seated)

Club Colours: Red & White striped shirts, red shorts
Nearest Railway Station: Brentford Central, South Ealing (tube)
Parking (Car): Street parking (restricted)
Parking (Coach/Bus): Layton Road car park
Police Force and Tel No: Metropolitan (0181 577 1212)
Disabled Visitors' Facilities
   Wheelchairs: Braemar Road
   Blind: Commentary available
Anticipated Development(s): Roof over Ealing Road End possible.

KEY
C Club Offices
S Club Shop
E Entrance(s) for visiting supporters
R Refreshment bars for visiting supporters
T Toilets for visiting supporters

↑ North direction (approx)

❶ Ealing Road
❷ Braemar Road
❸ Brook Road South
❹ To M4 (¹/4 mile) & South Ealing Tube Station (1 mile)
❺ Brentford Central BR Station
❻ To A315 High Street & Kew Bridge

Left: Brentford's Nicky Forster has been the subject of much Premier League attention following his season's high scoring. England U/21 recognition also followed for this livewire forward.

x

29

BRIGHTON & HOVE ALBION

Goldstone Ground, Newtown Road, Hove, Sussex, BN3 7DE

Tel No: 01273 778855
Advance Tickets Tel No: 01273 778855
League: 2nd Division
Brief History: Founded 1900 as Brighton and Hove Rangers, changed to Brighton and Hove Albion in 1902. Former Grounds: Home Farm (Withdean) and County Ground, moved to Goldstone Ground in 1902. Founder members Third Division (1920). Record attendance 36,747.
(Total) Current Capacity: 18,203 (5,274 seated)
Visiting Supporters' Allocation: 3,816 (738 seated)

Club Colours: Blue & white striped shirts, and matching shorts
Nearest Railway Station: Hove
Parking (Car): Greyhound Stadium and street parking
Parking (Coach/Bus): Conway Street
Police Force and Tel No: Sussex (01273 778922)
Disabled Visitors' Facilities
  Wheelchairs: Newtown Road (South West corner)
  Blind: Commentary available

KEY

C Club Offices
S Club Shop
E Entrance(s) for visiting supporters
R Refreshment bars for visiting supporters
T Toilets for visiting supporters

↑ North direction (approx)

❶ A27 Old Shoreham Road
❷ Nevill Road
❸ To A2038 & A23
❹ Goldstone Lane
❺ Newtown Road
❻ Greyhound Stadium
❼ Hove BR Station

Left: Pictured here in the Coca Cola Cup, and in Seagulls' change strip, are Kurt Nogan (before his departure to Burnley) and the cultured Stuart Munday.

BRISTOL CITY

Ashton Gate, Winterstoke Road, Ashton Road, Bristol, BS3 2EJ

Tel No: 0117 9632812
Advance Tickets Tel No: 0117 9632812
League: 2nd Division
Brief History: Founded 1894 as Bristol South End changed to Bristol City in 1897. Former Ground: St. John's Lane, Bedminster, moved to Ashton Gate in 1904. Record attendance 43,335
(Total) Current Capacity: 20,500 (all seated)
Club Colours: Red shirts, white shorts

Nearest Railway Station: Bristol Temple Meads
Parking (Car): Street parking
Parking (Coach/Bus): Marsh Road
Police Force and Tel No: Avon/Somerset (0117 9277777)
Disabled Visitors' Facilities
　Wheelchairs: Advanced notice not required
　Blind: Commentary available
Anticipated Development(s): Seats in Dolman Schoolboy's enclosure.

KEY
C Club Offices
S Club Shop
E Entrance(s) for visiting supporters

↑ North direction (approx)

❶ A370 Ashton Road
❷ A3209 Winterstoke Road
❸ To Temple Meads Station (1½ miles)
❹ To City Centre, A4, M32 & M4

Left: Even the efforts of 'Tanglefoot' Wayne Allison could not prevent City from returning to Division Two, when lack of goals proved to be the Robins' undoing.

BRISTOL ROVERS

Twerton Park, Bath, Avon

(Office: 199, Two Mile Hill Road, Kingswood, Bristol, BS15 1AZ)

Tel No: 0117 986 9999

Advance Tickets Tel No: 01225 312327

League: 2nd Division

Brief History: Founded 1883 as Black Arabs, changed to Eastville Rovers (1884), Bristol Eastville Rovers (1896) and Bristol Rovers in 1897. Former Grounds: Purdown, Three Acres, The Downs (Horfield), Ridgeway, Bristol Stadium (Eastville) moved to Twerton Park in 1986. Record attendance (at Eastville) 38,472. (At Twerton Park) 9,813.

(Total) Current Capacity: 8,800 (1,006 seated)

Visiting Supporters' Allocation: 1,125 (none seated)

Club Colours: Blue & white quartered shirts, white shorts

Nearest Railway Station: Bath Spa

Parking (Car): Street parking (limited)

Parking (Coach/Bus): Avon Street

Police Force and Tel No: Avon/Somerset (01225 444343)

Disabled Visitors' Facilities
  Wheelchairs: In front of Family stand
  Blind: Commentary available by arrangement

Anticipated Development(s): Hopeful future relocation to New Stadium at Severnside, Bristol.

KEY

E Entrance(s) for visiting supporters

R Refreshment bars for visiting supporters

T Toilets for visiting supporters

⬆ North direction (approx)

❶ High Street (Twerton)
❷ A36 Lower Bristol Road
❸ (Bath) City Centre & Bath Spa BR Station (1 1/2 miles)
❹ To Bristol
❺ River Avon

Left: Andy Tillson was one reason for a fine second half of the season in which Rovers almost gained promotion to Division One via the Play-Offs.

BURNLEY

Turf Moor, Brunshaw Road, Burnley, Lancs, BB10 4BX

Tel No: 01282 427777
Advance Tickets Tel No: 01282 427777
League: 2nd Division
Brief History: Founded 1882, Burnley Rovers (Rugby Club) combined with another Rugby Club, changed to soccer and name to Burnley. Moved from Calder Vale to Turf Moor in 1882. Founder-members Football League (1888). Record attendance 54,775.
(Total) Current Capacity: 22,966 (7,326 seated)
Club Colours: Claret with blue sleeved shirts, white shorts

Nearest Railway Station: Burnley Central

Parking (Car): Church Street and Fulledge Rec. (car parks)

Parking (Coach/Bus): As directed by Police

Police Force and Tel No: Lancashire (01282 425001)

Disabled Visitors' Facilities

Wheelchairs: Endsleigh Stand – Pre-match applications

Blind: Headsets provided with commentary.

KEY
C Club Offices
E Entrance(s) for visiting supporters

↑ North direction (approx)

❶ Brunshaw Road
❷ Belvedere Road
❸ Burnley Central BR Station (1/2 mile)
❹ Cricket Ground

Left: Jamie Hoyland looks
happy enough in this
Burnley away match
during November 1994, but
by the following May the
joy had turned to dismay
for relegation beckoned for
a team which could not
consolidate upon its
promotion of one year
earlier.

BURY

Gigg Lane, Bury, Lancashire, BL9 9HR

Tel No: 0161 764 4881
Advance Tickets Tel No: 0161 764 4881
League: 3rd Division
Brief History: Founded 1885, no former names or former grounds. Record attendance 35,000
(Total) Current Capacity: 12,900 to be confirmed (Currently 2,000 standing 9,600 seated)
Club Colours: White shirts, royal blue shorts

Nearest Railway Station: Bury Interchange
Parking (Car): Street parking
Parking (Coach/Bus): As directed by Police
Police Force and Tel No: Greater Manchester (0161 872 5050)
Disabled Visitors' Facilities
  Wheelchairs: South Stand
  Blind: Radio commentary (Press box)

KEY

C Club Offices
S Club Shop
E Entrance(s) for visiting supporters
R Refreshment bars for visiting supporters
T Toilets for visiting supporters

⬆ North direction (approx)

❶ Car Park
❷ Gigg Lane
❸ A56 Manchester Road
❹ Town Centre & Bury Interchange (Metrolink) (¾ mile)

Left: Mark Carter (facing the camera) proves a handful for Preston's Andy Fensome in this Division Three Play-off game, which was won by the Gigg Lane side.

CAMBRIDGE UNITED

Abbey Stadium, Newmarket Road, Cambridge, CB5 8LN

Tel No: 01223 566500
Advance Tickets Tel No: 01223 566500
League: 3rd Division
Brief History: Founded 1913 as Abbey United, changed to Cambridge United in 1949. Former Grounds: Midsummer Common, Stourbridge Common, Station Farm Barnwell (The Celery Trenches) & Parker's Piece, moved to Abbey Stadium in 1933. Record attendance 14,000.
(Total) Current Capacity: 10,100 (3,410 seated)

Visiting Supporters' Allocation: 2,266 (366 seated)
Club Colours: Amber shirts, black shorts
Nearest Railway Station: Cambridge (2 miles)
Parking (Car): Coldhams Common
Parking (Coach/Bus): Coldhams Common
Police Force and Tel No: Cambridge (01223 358966)
Disabled Visitors' Facilities
    Wheelchairs: 12 spaces
    Blind: No special facility

KEY

C Club Offices
S Club Shop
E Entrance(s) for visiting supporters
R Refreshment bars for visiting supporters
T Toilets for visiting supporters

↑ North direction (approx)

❶ A1134 Newmarket Road
❷ To A11 & Newmarket
❸ To City Centre, Cambridge BR Station (2 miles) & M11
❹ Whitehill Road

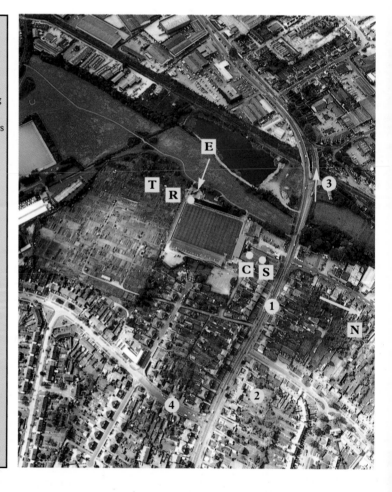

Left: Mick Heathcote of Cambridge United was the scorer of a vital goal against Champions-elect Birmingham City, but he was unable to prevent his side heading towards Division Three.

CARDIFF CITY

Ninian Park, Sloper Road, Cardiff, CF1 8SX

Tel No: 01222 398636
Advance Tickets Tel No: 01222 398636
League: 3rd Division
Brief History: Founded 1899. Former Grounds:
Riverside Cricket Club, Roath, Sophia
Gardens, Cardiff Arms Park & The Harlequins
Rugby Ground, moved to Ninian Park in 1910.
Ground record attendance 61,566 (Wales v.
England, 1961)
(Total) Current Capacity: 20,284 (12,598 seated)
Club Colours: Blue shirts, blue shorts
Nearest Railway Station: Ninian Park
(adjacent) (Cardiff Central 1 mile)

Parking (Car): Opposite Ground, no street
parking around ground
Parking (Coach/Bus): Sloper Road
Police Force and Tel No: South Wales (01222
222111)
Disabled Visitors' Facilities
Wheelchairs: Corner Canton Stand/Popular
Bank (covered)
Blind: No special facility
Anticipated Development(s): Popular Bank
(AKA 'The Bob Bank') to be converted to all
seater.

KEY

C Club Offices
E Entrance(s) for visiting supporters
R Refreshment bars for visiting supporters
T Toilets for visiting supporters (Terrace only, when used)

↑ North direction (approx)

❶ Sloper Road
❷ B4267 Leckwith Road
❸ Car Park
❹ To A4232 & M4 Junction 33 (8 miles)
❺ Ninian Park Road
❻ To City Centre & Cardiff Central BR Station (1 mile)
❼ To A48 Western Avenue, A48M, and M4 Junctions 32 and 29
❽ Ninian Park BR station

Left: Jason Perry hoists up his stocking during this Christmas 1994 match. Sadly for the 'Bluebirds', relegation to Division Three was the only present coming their way by the end of the season.

CARLISLE UNITED

Brunton Park, Warwick Road, Carlisle, CA1 1LL

Tel No: 01228 26237
Advance Tickets Tel No: 01228 26237
League: 2nd Division
Brief History: Founded 1904 as Carlisle United (previously named Shaddongate United). Former Grounds: Millholme Bank and Devonshire Park, moved to Brunton Park in 1909. Record attendance 27,500.
(Total) Current capacity: 17,500 (8,500 seated)
Visiting Supporters' Allocation: 1,105 (standing)

Club Colours: Royal blue shirts, white shorts
Nearest Railway Station: Carlisle Citadel
Parking (Car): Rear of ground
Parking (Coach/Bus): St. Aiden's Road car park
Police Force and Tel No: Cumbria (01228 28191)
Disabled Visitors' Facilities
  Wheelchairs: Front of Main Stand (prior arrangement)
  Blind: Commentary available

KEY

C Club Offices
E Entrance(s) for visiting supporters
R Refreshment bars for visiting supporters
T Toilets for visiting supporters

↑ North direction (approx)

❶ A69 Warwick Road
❷ M6 Junction 43
❸ Carlisle Citadel BR Station (1 mile)
❹ Greystone Road
❺ Car Park

Left: Paul Conway celebrates the Cumbrian's third goal against Fulham, during their runaway promotion campaign.

CHARLTON ATHLETIC

The Valley, Floyd Road, Charlton, London, SE7 8BL

Tel No: 0181 293 4567
Advance Tickets Tel No: 0181 293 4567
League: 1st Division
Brief History: Founded 1905. Former grounds: Siemens Meadows, Woolwich Common, Pound Park, Angerstein Athletic Ground, The Mount Catford, Selhurst Park (Crystal Palace FC), Boleyn Ground (West Ham United FC), The Valley (1919-1923, 1924-85, 1992-). Founder Members 3rd Division South. Record attendance 75,031.

(Total) Current Capacity: 14,203 all seated
Club Colours: Red shirts, white shorts
Nearest Railway Station: Charlton
Parking (Car): Street parking
Parking (Coach/Bus): As directed by Police
Police Force and Tel No: Metropolitan (0181 853 8212)
Disabled Visitors' Facilities
  Wheelchairs: East/West Stands
  Blind: Commentary, 12 spaces.

KEY

C Club Offices
E Entrance(s) for visiting supporters

↑ North direction (approx)

❶ Harvey Gardens
❷ A206 Woolwich Road
❸ Valley Grove
❹ Floyd Road
❺ Charlton BR Station
❻ River Thames
❼ Thames Barrier

Left: Paul Mortimer now seems to be an established member of the Charlton side, and perhaps his trusty left foot can inspire the side to greater things in the 1995/96 season.

CHELSEA

Stamford Bridge, Fulham Road, London, SW6 1HS

Tel No: 0171 385 5545
Advance Tickets Tel No: 0171 385 5545
League: F.A. Premier
Brief History: Founded 1905. Admitted to Football League (2nd Division) on formation. Stamford Bridge venue for F.A. Cup Finals 1919-1922. Record attendance 82,905.
(Total) Current capacity: 25,738 (all seated)
Visiting Supporters' Allocation: Approx. 1,750
Club Colours: Blue shirts, blue shorts
Nearest Railway Station: Fulham Broadway

Parking (Car): Street parking
Parking (Coach/Bus): As directed by Police
Police Force and Tel No: Metropolitan (0171 385 1212)
Disabled Visitors' Facilities
  Wheelchairs: East Stand
  Blind: No special facility
Anticipated Development(s): (Editor's note: Update information regarding ground not advised)

KEY

C Club Offices
S Club Shop
E Entrance(s) for visiting supporters

↑ North direction (approx)

❶ A308 Fulham Road
❷ Central London
❸ Fulham Broadway Tube Station

48

Left: Chelsea's international central defender, Erland Johnson, attempts to calm things down in a late 1994/95 season fixture at Stamford Bridge.

CHESTER CITY

The Deva Stadium, Bumpers Lane, Chester

Tel No: 01244 371376
Advance Tickets Tel No: 01244 373829
Commercial: 01244 390243
League: 3rd Division
Brief History: Founded 1884 from amalgamation of Chester Wanderers and Chester Rovers. Former Grounds: Faulkner Street, Lightfoot Street, Whipcord Lane, Sealand Road, Moss Rose (Macclesfield Town F.C.), moved to Deva Stadium in 1992. Record attendance (Sealand Road) 20,500.
(Total) Current Capacity: 6,000 (3,408 seated)

Visiting Supporters' Allocation: 1,933 max (seated 637 max.)
Club Colours: Blue/White striped shirts, Black shorts
Nearest Railway Station: Chester (3 miles)
Parking (Car): Car park at ground
Parking (Coach/Bus): Car park at ground
Police Force and Tel No: Cheshire (01244 350222)
Disabled Visitors' Facilities
 Wheelchairs: West and East Stand
 Blind: Facility available

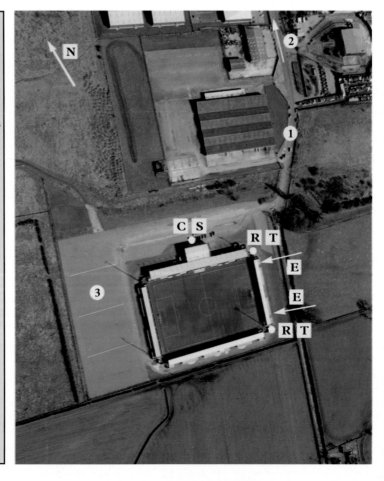

KEY
C Club Offices
S Club Shop
E Entrance(s) for visiting supporters
R Refreshment bars for visiting supporters
T Toilets for visiting supporters

↑ North direction (approx)

❶ Bumpers Lane
❷ To City Centre and Chester BR Station (1 1/2 miles)
❸ Car Park

Left: Relegation seemed the only outcome for City from the early days of the 1994/95 season. One of the positive things to have come from a wretched season, was the consistency of Gary Hackett, pictured here.

CHESTERFIELD

Recreation Ground, Saltergate, Chesterfield, S40 4SX

Tel No: 01246 209765
Advance Tickets Tel No: 01246 209765
League: 2nd Division
Brief History: Founded 1866. Former Ground: Spital Vale. Formerly named Chesterfield Town. Record attendance 30,968
(Total) Current Capacity: 11,308 (2,608 Seated)
Club Colours: Blue and white striped shirts, white shorts
Nearest Railway Station: Chesterfield

Parking (Car): Saltergate car park, street parking
Parking (Coach/Bus): As directed by Police
Police Force and Tel No: Derbyshire (01246 220100)
Disabled Visitors' Facilities
  Wheelchairs: Saltergate Stand
  Blind: No special facility
Anticipated Development(s): (Editor's note: Updated information regarding ground not advised)

KEY

C Club Offices
S Club Shop
E Entrance(s) for visiting supporters
R Refreshment bars for visiting supporters
T Toilets for visiting supporters

 North direction (approx)

❶ Saltergate
❷ Cross Street
❸ St Margaret's Drive
❹ A632 West Bars
❺ To A617 & M1 Junction 29

Left: Tony Lormor is seen in action during the Third Division Play-Off final on Saturday 27 May. Promotion to the 2nd Division marked a successful end to the club's season.

COLCHESTER UNITED

Layer Road Ground, Colchester, CO2 7JJ

Tel No: 01206 574042
Advance Tickets Tel No: 01206 574042
League: 3rd Division
Brief History: Founded 1937, joined Football League 1950, relegated 1990, promoted 1992. Record attendance 19,072.
(Total) Current Capacity: 7,944 (1,150 Seated)
Club Colours: Royal Blue shirts, White shorts

Nearest Railway Station: Colchester Town
Parking (Car): Street parking
Parking (Coach/Bus): Boadicea Way
Police Force and Tel No: Essex (01206 762212)
Disabled Visitor' Facilities
  Wheelchairs: Space for six in front of terrace (next to Main Stand)
  Blind: Space for 3 blind persons and 3 guiders.

KEY
- **C** Club Offices
- **S** Club Shop
- **E** Entrance(s) for visiting supporters
- **R** Refreshment bars for visiting supporters
- **T** Toilets for visiting supporters

↑ North direction (approx)

❶ B1026 Layer Road
❷ Town Centre & Colchester Town BR Station (2 miles)
❸ Main Stand
❹ Popular Side

54

Left: U's former Arsenal hopeful Gus Caesar (in blue and white stripes) seems to be dancing the tango with Hereford's Neil Lyne in this League encounter.

COVENTRY CITY

Highfield Stadium, King Richard Street, Coventry CV2 4FW.

Tel No: 01203 223535

Advance Tickets Tel No: 01203 225545

League: F.A. Premier

Brief History: Founded 1883 as Singers F.C., changed name to Coventry City in 1898. Former grounds; Dowell's Field, Stoke Road Ground, moved to Highfield Road in 1899. Record attendance, 51,455.

(Total) Current Capacity: 22,600 all seated

Visiting Supporters' Allocation: 4,082 all seated

Club Colours: Sky blue shirts, sky blue shorts.

Nearest Railway Station: Coventry.

Parking (Car): Street parking

Parking (Coach/Bus): Gosford Green Coach Park.

Police Force and Tel No: West Midlands (01203 539010)

Disabled Visitors' Facilities

Wheelchairs: Clock Stand (Plus future-section of the East Stand)

Blind: Clock Stand (booking necessary)

KEY

C Club Offices

S Club Shop

E Entrance(s) for visiting supporters

R Refreshment bars for visiting supporters

T Toilets for visiting supporters

↑ North direction (approx)

❶ Swan Lane
❷ A4600 Walsgrave Road
❸ Thackhall Street
❹ Coventry BR Station (1 mile)
❺ To M6 Junction 2 and M69
❻ To M45 Junction 1
❼ Gosford Green Coach Park

Left: Coventry's Zimbabwe International Peter Ndlovu seen in typical fleetfooted action on Boxing Day 1994. On his day, he is one of the most exciting players in English football.

CREWE ALEXANDRA

Gresty Road Ground, Crewe, Cheshire, CW2 6EB

Tel No: 01270 213014

Advance Tickets Tel No: 01270 213014

League: 2nd Division

Brief History: Founded 1877. Former Grounds; Alexandra Recreation ground (Nantwich Road), Earle Street Cricket Ground, Edleston Road, Old Sheds Fields, Gresty Road (Adjacent to current Ground), moved to current Ground in 1906. Founder members of 2nd Division (1892) until 1896. Founder members of 3rd Division North (1921). Record attendance 20,000.

(Total) Current Capacity: 5,800 (4,700 seated)

Visiting Supporters' Allocation: 1,000

Club Colours: Red Shirts, White Shorts.

Nearest Railway Station: Crewe.

Parking (Car): Car Park near Ground

Parking (Coach/Bus): Car Park near Ground

Police Force and Tel No: Cheshire (01270 500222)

Disabled Visitors' Facilities
  Wheelchairs: In visitors stand
  Blind: Commentary available

KEY

C Club Offices
S Club Shop
E Entrance(s) for visiting supporters
R Refreshment bars for visiting supporters
T Toilets for visiting supporters

↑ North direction (approx)

❶ Crewe BR Station
❷ Car Park
❸ Gresty Road
❹ A534 Nantwich Road
❺ A5020 to M6 Junction 16
❻ To M6 Junction 17

Left: Danny Murphy exhibits the creative principles preached by Crewe Manager Dario Gradi. What a shame that this fine passing side must continue to sell in order to survive.

CRYSTAL PALACE

Selhurst Park, London, SE25 6PY

Tel No: 0181 653 1000
Advance Tickets Tel No: 0181 771 8841
League: 1st Division
Brief History: Founded 1905. Former Grounds: The Crystal Palace (F.A. Cup Finals venue), London County Athletic Ground (Herne Hill), The Nest (Croydon Common Athletic Ground), moved to Selhurst Park in 1924. Founder members 3rd Division (1920). Record attendance 51,482.
(Total) Current Capacity: 26,000 all seated
Visiting Supporters' Allocation: Approx 2,500
Club Colours: Red with blue striped shirts, red shorts

Nearest Railway Station: Selhurst, Norwood Junction & Thornton Heath

Parking (Car): Street parking & Sainsbury's car park

Parking (Coach/Bus): Thornton Heath

Police Force and Tel No: Metropolitan (0181 653 8568)

Disabled Visitors' Facilities
 Wheelchairs: Park Road Stand (limited)
 Blind: Commentary available

Anticipated Development(s): New stand, Holmesdale Road, End, opening August 1995.

KEY
C Club Offices
S Club Shop
E Entrance(s) for visiting supporters
T Toilets for visiting supporters

↑ North direction (approx)

❶ Whitehorse Lane
❷ Park Road
❸ A213 Selhurst Road
❹ Selhurst BR Station (1/2 mile)
❺ Norwood Junction BR Station (1/4 mile)
❻ Thornton Heath BR Station (1/2 mile)
❼ Car Park (Sainsbury's)

Left: Chris Armstrong bore the brunt of much criticism from manager Alan Smith following his drugs nightmare last season, but neither were able to save Palace from the big drop. Both have now departed to pastures new; Armstong to Spurs.

DARLINGTON

Feethams Ground, Darlington, DL1 5JB

Tel No: 01325 465097
Advance Tickets Tel No: 01325 465097
League: 3rd Division
Brief History: Founded 1883. Founder Members of 3rd Division North (1921), Relegated from 4th Division (1989). Promoted from GM Vauxhall Conference in 1990. Record attendance 21,023.
(Total) Current Capacity: 7,046 (1,120 seated)
Visiting Supporters' Allocation: 1,200 (250 seated)

Club Colours: White and Black Shirts, Black Shorts.
Nearest Railway Station: Darlington
Parking (Car): Street parking
Parking (Coach/Bus): As directed by Police
Police Force and Tel No: Durham (01325 467681)
Disabled Visitors' Facilities
  Wheelchairs: East Stand (free entrance)
  Blind: By prior arrangement

KEY

C Club Offices
S Club Shop
E Entrance(s) for visiting supporters
R Refreshment bars for visiting supporters
T Toilets for visiting supporters

↑ North direction (approx)

❶ Polam Lane
❷ Victoria Embankment
❸ Feethams Cricket Ground
❹ Victoria Road
❺ Darlington BR Station (¼ mile)
❻ To A1 (M)

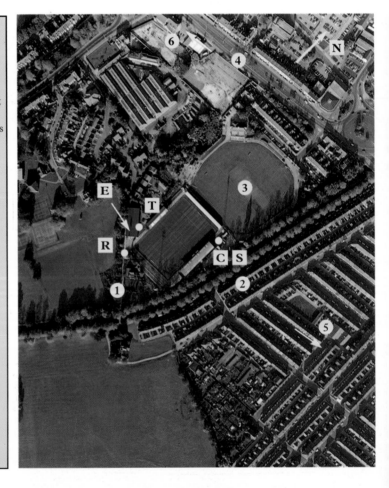

Left: The Quakers' keeper, Darren Collier, looks in pensive mood as he watches the action in a League Division 3 game.

DERBY COUNTY

Baseball Ground, Shaftesbury Crescent, Derby, DE3 8NB

Tel No: 01332 340105
Advance Tickets Tel No: 01332 340105
League: 1st Division
Brief History: Founded 1884. Former Ground: The Racecourse Ground, moved to Baseball Ground in 1894. Founder-members of the Football League (1888). Record attendance 41,826.
(Total) Current Capacity: 19,500 (14,800 seated)
Club Colours: White shirts, black shorts
Nearest Railway Station: Derby Midland and Ramsline Halt (specials)

Parking (Car): Several car parks

Parking (Coach/Bus): Russel Street

Police Force and Tel No: Derbyshire (01332 290100)

Disabled Visitors' Facilities
 Wheelchairs: Vulcan Street
 Blind: Commentary available

Anticipated Development(s): (Editor's note: Update information regarding Ground not advised.)

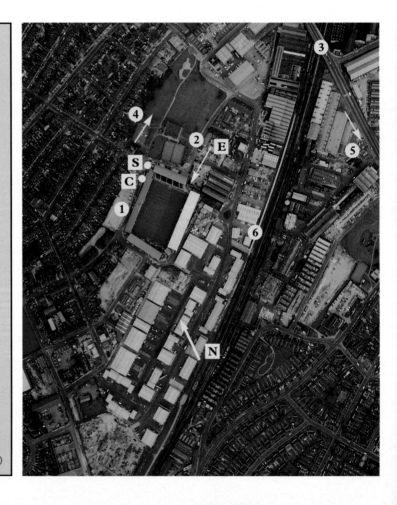

KEY
C Club Offices
S Club Shop
E Entrance(s) for visiting supporters

⬆ North direction (approx)

❶ Shaftesbury Crescent
❷ Colombo Street
❸ A514 Osmaston Road
❹ To Derby Midland BR Station (1 mile)
❺ To Ring Road, A6 & M1 Junction 24
❻ Ramsline Halt (BR Specials)

Left: At last Craig Short is showing that his expensive move from Notts County is paying off, and proving to Rams fans what a quality central defender he is.

DONCASTER ROVERS

Belle Vue, Bawtry Road, Doncaster DN4 5HT

Tel No: 01302 539441
Advance Tickets Tel No: 01302 539441
League: 3rd Division
Brief History: Founded 1879. Former Grounds: Town Moor, Belle Vue (not current Ground), Deaf School Playing Field (later name Intake Ground), Bennetthorpe, moved to Belle Vue (former name Low Pasture) in 1922. Record attendance 37,099.

(Total) Current Capacity: 6,535 (1,259 seated)

Club Colours: White with Red trim Shirts, White Shorts.
Nearest Railway Station: Doncaster
Parking (Car): Car Park at ground
Parking (Coach/Bus): Car Park at ground
Police Force and Tel No: South Yorkshire (01302 366744)
Disabled Visitors' Facilities
  Wheelchairs: Bawtry Road
  Blind: No special facility

KEY

C Club Offices
S Club Shop
E Entrance(s) for visiting supporters
R Refreshment bars for visiting supporters
T Toilets for visiting supporters

↑ North direction (approx)

❶ A638 Bawtry Road
❷ Racecourse
❸ Car Park
❹ To Doncaster BR Station & A1(M) (3 miles)
❺ To A630 & M18 Junction 4

Left: The well-built ex-Stockport County player, tough tackling Gary Brabin was unable to secure for the Rovers the play-off spot they threatened for most of the 1994/95 season.

EVERTON

Goodison Park, Goodison Road, Liverpool, L4 4EL

Tel No: 0151 521 2020
Advance Tickets Tel No: 0151 521 2020
Dial a Seat: 0151 525 1231
League: FA Premier
Brief History: Founded 1879 as St. Domingo, changed to Everton in 1880. Former Grounds: Stanley Park, Priory Road and Anfield (Liverpool F.C. Ground), moved to Goodison Park in 1892. Founder-members Football League (1888). Record attendance 78,229.
(Total) Current Capacity: 40,000 all seated

Club Colours: Blue shirts, white shorts
Nearest Railway Station: Liverpool Lime Street
Parking (Car): Corner of Utting & Priory Avenues
Parking (Coach/Bus): Priory Road
Police Force and Tel No: Merseyside (0151 709 6010)
Disabled Visitors' Facilities
  Wheelchairs: Park End Stand.
  Blind: Commentary available

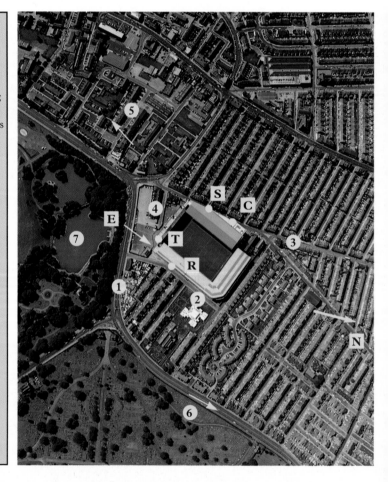

KEY

C Club Offices
S Club Shop
E Entrance(s) for visiting supporters
R Refreshment bars for visiting supporters
T Toilets for visiting supporters

↑ North direction (approx)

❶ A580 Walton Road
❷ Bullens Road
❸ Goodison Road
❹ Car Park
❺ Liverpool Lime Street BR Station (2 miles)
❻ To M57 Junction 2, 4 and 5
❼ Stanley Park

Right: Daniel Amokachi, once nicknamed 'Amotaxi' (black, expensive and carrying lots of passengers) following his move from the continent, is now a firm favourite for the Cup winners.

EXETER CITY

St. James Park, Exeter, EX4 6PX

Tel No: 01392 54073

Advance Tickets Tel No: 01392 54073

League: 3rd Division

Brief History: Founded in 1904. (From amalgamation of St. Sidwell United and Exeter United.) Founder-members Third Division (1920). Record attendance 20,984.

(Total) Current Capacity: 10,186 (1,608 seated)

Club Colours: Red and white striped shirts, white shorts

Nearest Railway Station: Exeter St. James Park

Parking (Car): National Car Park and Council Car Parks (No street parking)

Parking (Coach/Bus): Paris Street bus station

Police Force and Tel No: Devon and Cornwall (01392 52101)

Disabled Visitors' Facilities
Wheelchairs: St. James Road entrance (prior booking)
Blind: No special facility

Anticipated Development(s): Possible relocation in 1996/97.

KEY

C Club Offices
S Club Shop
E Entrance(s) for visiting supporters
T Toilets for visiting supporters

↑ North direction (approx)

❶ Exeter St. James Park BR Station
❷ St. James Road
❸ Old Tiverton Road
❹ Blackboy Road

Right: City's Martin Phillips seen in action during August 1994; at this stage the team was no doubt unaware of the club's financial worries that were to become a feature during the season.

FULHAM

Craven Cottage, Stevenage Road, Fulham, London, SW6 6HH

Tel No: 0171 736 6561

Advance Tickets Tel No: 0171 736 6561

League: 3rd Division

Brief History: Founded in 1879 as St. Andrews Fulham, changed name to Fulham in 1898. Former Grounds: Star Road, Ranelagh Club, Lillie Road, Eel Brook Common, Purser's Cross, Barn Elms and Half Moon (Wasps Rugby Football Ground), moved to Craven Cottage in 1894. Record attendance 49,335.

(Total) Current Capacity: 14,542 (4,652 seated)

Club Colours: White shirts, black shorts

Nearest Railway Station: Putney Bridge (Tube)

Parking (Car): Street parking

Parking (Coach/Bus): Stevenage Road

Police Force and Tel No: Metropolitan (0171 741 6212)

Disabled Visitors' Facilities

Wheelchairs: Miller Stand

Blind: Commentary available (prior arrangement)

KEY

C Club Offices (The Cottage)

S Club Shop

E Entrance(s) for visiting supporters

R Refreshment bars for visiting supporters

T Toilets for visiting supporters

↑ North direction (approx)

❶ River Thames

❷ Stevenage Road

❸ Finlay Street

❹ Putney Bridge Tube Station (1/2 mile)

Left: Terry Hurlock, now in the twilight of his much travelled playing career – which started and now continues in London – points the way for his Craven Cottage team-mates.

GILLINGHAM

Priestfield Stadium, Redfern Avenue, Gillingham, Kent, ME7 4DD

Tel No: 01634 851854
Advance Tickets Tel No: 01634 576828
League: 3rd Division
Brief History: Founded 1893, as New Brompton, changed name to Gillingham in 1913. Founder-members Third Division (1920). Lost Football League status (1938), re-elected to Third Division South (1950). Record attendance 23,002.
(Total) Current Capacity: 10,422 (1,225 seated)

Club Colours: Blue shirts, white shorts
Nearest Railway Station: Gillingham
Parking (Car): Street parking
Parking (Coach/Bus): As directed by Police
Police Force and Tel No: Kent (01634 834488)
Disabled Visitors' Facilities
  Wheelchairs: Redfern Avenue
  Blind: No special facility

KEY

C Club Offices
S Club Shop
E Entrance(s) for visiting supporters
R Refreshment bars for visiting supporters
T Toilets for visiting supporters

↑ North direction (approx)

❶ Redfern Avenue
❷ Toronto Road
❸ Gordon Road
❹ Gillingham BR Station (¼ mile)
❺ Woodlands Road

Right: 1994/95 was a much troubled season for Gillingham. Here, Neil Smith flies down the wing in this April 1995 Division Three encounter.

GRIMSBY TOWN

Blundell Park, Cleethorpes, DN35 7PY

Tel No: 01472 697111
Advance Tickets Tel No: 01472 697111
League: 1st Division
Brief History: Founded 1878, as Grimsby Pelham, changed name to Grimsby Town in 1879. Former Grounds: Clee Park (two adjacent fields) & Abbey Park, moved to Blundell Park in 1899. Founder-members 2nd Division (1892). Record attendance 31,651.
(Total) Current Capacity: Approx. 8,000 (all seated)

Club Colours: Black & white striped shirts, black shorts
Nearest Railway Station: Cleethorpes & New Clee (specials)
Parking (Car): Street Parking
Parking (Coach/Bus): Harrington Street
Police Force and Tel No: Humberside (01472 359171)
Disabled Visitors' Facilities
  Wheelchairs: Harrington Street
  Blind: Commentary available

KEY

C Club Offices (Findus Stand)
S Club Shop
E Entrance(s) for visiting supporters
R Refreshment bars for visiting supporters
T Toilets for visiting supporters

↑ North direction (approx)

❶ A180 Grimsby Road
❷ Cleethorpes BR Station (1½ miles)
❸ To Grimsby and M180 Junction 5
❹ Harrington Street
❺ Constitutional Avenue
❻ Humber Estuary

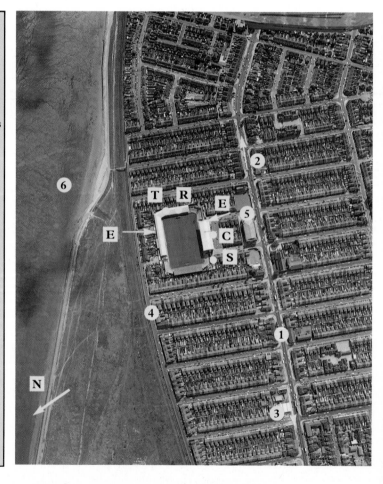

Left: Paul Groves epitomises the quality passing football that is now a fixture at Blundell Park. Here he glides forward in search of another Grimsby Goal.

HARTLEPOOL UNITED

Victoria Ground, Clarence Road, Hartlepool, TS24 8BZ

Tel No: 01429 272584
Advance Tickets Tel No: 01429 222077
League: 3rd Division
Brief History: Founded 1908 as Hartlepools United, changed to Hartlepool (1968) and to Hartlepool United in 1977. Founder-members 3rd Division (1921). Record attendance 17,426.
(Total) Current capacity: 7,061 anticipated (3,616 seated)
Visiting Supporters' Allocation: 680 (allocation can be extended to 2,070)

Club Colours: Blue & white striped shirts, Blue shorts
Nearest Railway Station: Hartlepool Church Street
Parking (car): Street parking and rear of clock garage
Police Force and Tel No: Cleveland (01429 221151)
Disabled Visitors' Facilities
  Wheelchairs: Raby Road
  Blind: Commentary available

KEY
C Club Offices
S Club Shop
E Entrance(s) for visiting supporters

↑ North direction (approx)

❶ A1088 Clarence Road
❷ Hartlepool Church Street BR Station
❸ A179 Raby Road
❹ Greyhound Stadium
❺ To Middlesbrough A689 & A1(M)

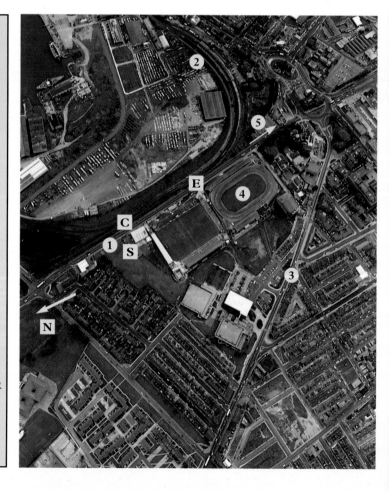

Right: Hartlepool's Nicky Southall is seen in FA Cup action on 12 November 1994.

HEREFORD UNITED

Edgar Street, Hereford, HR4 9JU

Tel No: 01432 276666
Advance Tickets Tel No: 01432 276666
League: 3rd Division
Brief History: Founded 1924, elected to Football League 1972. Record attendance 18,114
(Total) Current Capacity: 13,777 (2,897 seated)
Club Colours: White shirts, black shorts

Nearest Railway Station: Hereford
Parking (Car): Merton Meadow & Edgar Street
Parking (Coach/Bus): Cattle Market
Police Force and Tel No: Hereford (01432 276422)
Disabled Visitors' Facilities
  Wheelchairs: Edgar Street (few)
  Blind: Commentary available

KEY

- **C** Club Offices
- **S** Club Shop
- **E** Entrance(s) for visiting supporters
- **R** Refreshment bars for visiting supporters
- **T** Toilets for visiting supporters

↑ North direction (approx)

❶ A49 Edgar Street
❷ Blackfriars Street
❸ Hereford BR Station (½ mile)
❹ Newmarket Street
❺ To A438 & M50

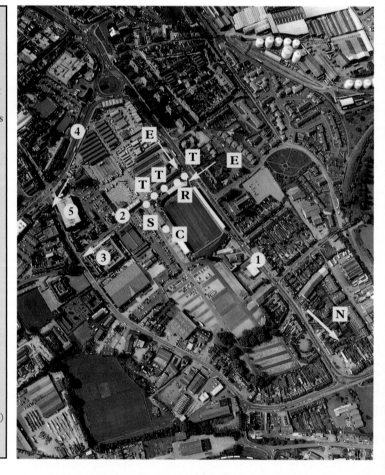

Left: Hereford's Mark Fishlock pictured during a League encounter at Edgar Street during April 1995.

HUDDERSFIELD TOWN

The Alfred McAlpine Stadium, Leeds Road, Huddersfield, HD1 6PX

Tel No: 01484 420335

Advance Tickets Tel No: 01484 420335

League: 1st Division

Brief History: Founded 1908, elected to Football League in 1910. First Club to win the Football League Championship three years in succession. Moved from Leeds Road ground to Kirklees (Alfred McAlpine) Stadium 1994/95 season. Record attendance (Leeds Road) 67,037.

(Total) Current Capacity: 19,300 (all seated)

Visiting Supporters' Allocation: 4,037 (all seated)

Club Colours: Blue and white striped shirts, white shorts

Nearest Railway Station: Huddersfield

Parking (Car): Car parks adjacent to ground

Parking (Coach/Bus): Car parks adjacent to ground

Police Force and Tel No: West Yorkshire (01484 422122)

Disabled Visitors' Facilities
 Wheelchairs: Three sides of Ground, at low levels and raised areas, including toilets access.
 Blind: Area for Partially sighted with Hospital Radio commentary.

KEY

- **C** Club Offices
- **S** Club Shop
- **E** Entrance(s) for visiting supporters
- **R** Refreshment bars for visiting supporters
- **T** Toilets for visiting supporters

↑ North direction (approx)

- ❶ To Leeds and M62 Junction 25
- ❷ A62 Leeds Road
- ❸ To Huddersfield BR station (1¹⁄₄ miles)
- ❹ Disabled parking
- ❺ Town Avenue pay car park (on site of former ground)
- ❻ Bradley Mills (permit only car park)
- ❼ St Andrews pay car park
- ❽ Coach park

Right: Central defender, and ex-Mansfield Town man, Kevin Gray made his contribution towards Huddersfield's eventual move up from Division Two.

HULL CITY

Boothferry Park, Boothferry Road, Hull, HU4 6EU

Tel No: 01482 51119
Advance Tickets Tel No: 01482 51119
League: 2nd Division
Brief History: Founded 1904. Former grounds: The Boulevard (Hull Rugby League Ground), Dairycoates, Anlaby Road Cricket Circle (Hull Cricket Ground), Anlaby Road, moved to Boothferry Park in 1946. Record attendance 55,019.
(Total) Current Capacity: 17,208 (5,515 seated)
Visiting Supporters' Allocation: 2,960 (530 seated)

Club Colours: Amber & black striped shirts, black shorts
Nearest Railway Station: Hull Paragon
Parking (Car): Street Parking and at ground (limited)
Parking (Coach/Bus): At ground
Police Force and Tel No: Humberside (01482 220148)
Disabled Visitors' Facilities
   Wheelchairs: Corner East/South stands
   Blind: Commentary available

KEY

C Club Offices
E Entrance(s) for visiting supporters

↑ North direction (approx)

❶ A63 Boothferry Road
❷ North Road
❸ Hull Paragon BR Station (1½ miles)
❹ To Humber Bridge and M62 Junction 38

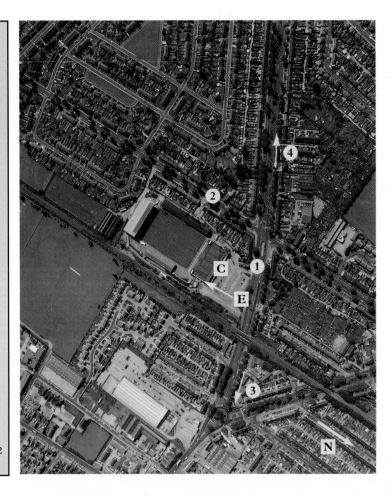

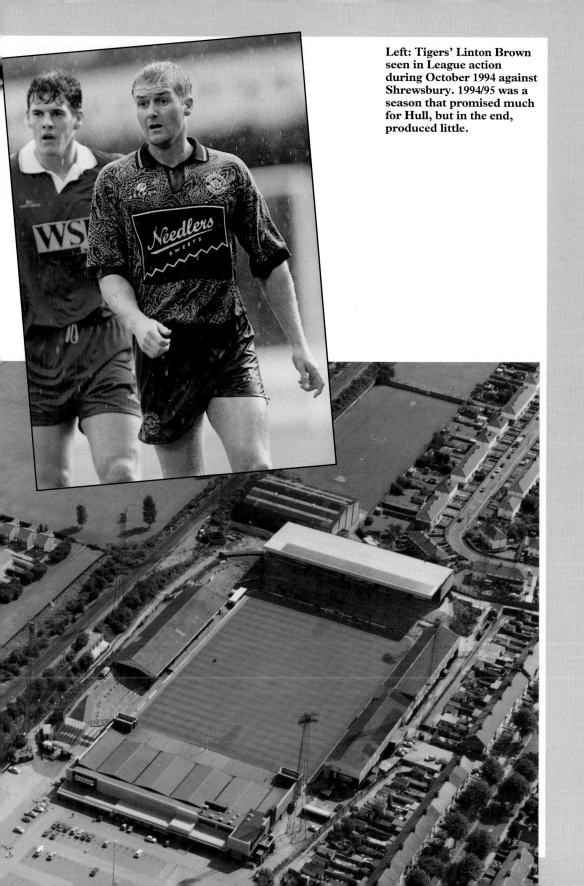

Left: Tigers' Linton Brown seen in League action during October 1994 against Shrewsbury. 1994/95 was a season that promised much for Hull, but in the end, produced little.

IPSWICH TOWN

Portman Road, Ipswich, IP1 2DA

Tel No: 01473 219211

Advance Tickets Tel No: 01473 221133

League: 1st Division

Brief History: Founded 1887 as Ipswich Association F.C., changed to Ipswich Town in 1888. Former Grounds: Broom Hill & Brookes Hall, moved to Portman Road in 1888. Record attendance 38,010

(Total) Current Capacity: 22,500 all seated

Visiting Supporters Allocation: 1,500 seated

Club Colours: Blue shirts, white shorts

Nearest Railway Station: Ipswich

Parking (Car): Portman Road, Portman Walk & West End Road

Parking (Coach/Bus): West End Road

Police Force and Tel No: Suffolk (01473 611611)

Disabled Visitors' Facilities
Wheelchairs: South Stand (Churchmans)
Blind: Commentary available

KEY

C Club Offices
S Club Shop
E Entrance(s) for visiting supporters
R Refreshment bars for visiting supporters
T Toilets for visiting supporters

↑ North direction (approx)

❶ A137 West End Road
❷ Portman Walk
❸ Portman Road
❹ Princes Street
❺ Ipswich BR Station
❻ Car Parks

Left: Steve Sedgley moved to East Anglia from 'Spurs in 1994, and must wonder what he's done wrong following Town's relegation. A quality player who will probably be playing at the top level again.

LEEDS UNITED

Elland Road, Leeds, LS11 0ES

Tel No: 0113 271 6037
Advance Tickets Tel No: 0113 271 0710
League: F.A. Premier
Brief History: Founded 1919, formed from the former 'Leeds City' Club, who were disbanded following expulsion from the Football League in October 1919. Joined Football League in 1920. Record attendance 57,892
(Total) Current Capacity: 39,800 (all seated)
Club Colours: White shirts, white shorts

Nearest Railway Station: Leeds City

Parking (Car): Car parks adjacent to ground

Parking (Coach/Bus): As directed by Police

Police Force and Tel No: West Yorkshire (0113 243 5353)

Disabled Visitors' Facilities

Wheelchairs: West Stand and South Stand

Blind: Commentary available

KEY

C Club Offices
S Club Shop
E Entrance(s) for visiting supporters

↑ North direction (approx)

❶ M621
❷ M621 Junction 2
❸ A643 Elland Road
❹ Lowfields Road
❺ To A58

Right: Leeds' left back Tony Dorigo – many observers still cannot understand why this outstanding defender does not feature in the current International set-up.

LEICESTER CITY

City Stadium, Filbert Street, Leicester, LE2 7FL

Tel No: 0116 255 5000

Advance Tickets Tel No: 0116 255 5000

League: 1st Division

Brief History: Founded 1884 as Leicester Fosse, changed name to Leicester City in 1919. Former Grounds: Fosse Road South, Victoria Road, Belgrave Cycle Track, Mill Lane & Aylestone Road Cricket Ground, moved to Filbert Street in 1891. Record attendance 47,298

(Total) Current Capacity: 21,500 (all seated)

Visiting Supporters' Allocation: approx 1,800

Club Colours: Blue shirts, blue shorts

Nearest Railway Station: Leicester

Parking (Car): NCP car park & street parking

Parking (Coach/Bus): Western Boulevard

Police Force and Tel No: Leicester (0116 253 0066)

Disabled Visitors' Facilities
  Wheelchairs: Filbert Street
  Blind: No special facility

KEY

C Club Offices

S Club Shop

E Entrance(s) for visiting supporters

R Refreshment bars for visiting supporters

T Toilets for visiting supporters

↑ North direction (approx)

❶ Walnut Street
❷ Filbert Street
❸ Grasmere Street
❹ River Soar
❺ M1 and M69 Junction 21
❻ Leicester BR Station (1 mile)

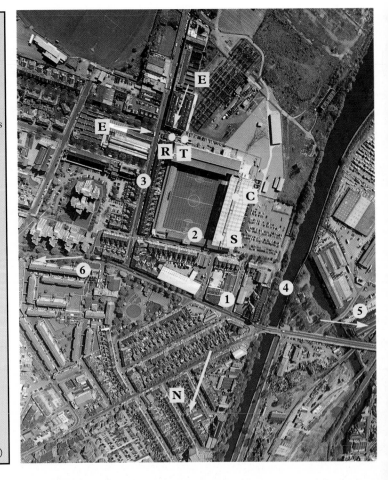

Right: Julian Joachim of Leicester City is something of an enigma; on his day he is an exciting and devastating winger. Perhaps a move is in store following City's relegation from the top-flight?

LEYTON ORIENT

Leyton Stadium, Brisbane Road, Leyton, London, E10 5NE

Tel No: 0181 539 2223
Advance Tickets Tel No: 0181 539 2223
League: 3rd Division
Brief History: Founded 1887 as Clapton Orient, from Eagle Cricket Club (formerly Glyn Cricket Club formed in 1881). Changed name to Leyton Orient (1946), Orient (1966), Leyton Orient (1987). Former grounds: Glyn Road, Whittles Athletic Ground, Millfields Road, Lea Bridge Road, Wembley Stadium (2 games), moved to Brisbane Road in 1937. Record attendance 34,345.

(Total) Current Capacity: 18,869 (7,171 Seated)
Club Colours: Red shirts, white shorts
Nearest Railway Station: Leyton (tube), Leyton Midland Road
Parking (Car): Street parking
Parking (Coach/Bus): As directed by Police
Police Force and Tel No: Metropolitan (0181 556 8855)
Disabled Visitors Facilities
   Wheelchairs: Windsor Road
   Blind: Match commentary supplied on request

KEY

C Club Offices
S Club Shop
E Entrance(s) for visiting supporters
R Refreshment bars for visiting supporters
T Toilets for visiting supporters

⬆ North direction (approx)

❶ Buckingham Road
❷ Oliver Road
❸ A112 High Road Leyton
❹ Leyton Tube Station (¼ mile)
❺ Brisbane Road

Left: O's Kevin Austin patrols the fine Brisbane Road pitch in an early 1994/95 season home League fixture. However, a poor season for Orient culminated in the drop to the basement division.

LINCOLN CITY

Sincil Bank, Lincoln, LN5 8LD

Tel No: 01522 522224

Advance Tickets Tel No: 01522 522224

League: 3rd Division

Brief History: Founded 1884. Former Ground: John O'Gaunts Ground, moved to Sincil Bank in 1895. Founder-members 2nd Division Football League (1892). Relegated from 4th Division in 1987, promoted from GM Vauxhall Conference in 1988. Record attendance 23,196.

(Total) Current Capacity: 10,918 (9,246 seated)

Visiting Supporters' Allocation: 1,585 (all seated)

Club Colours: Red & white striped shirts, black shorts

Nearest Railway Station: Lincoln Central

Parking (Car): Adjacent Ground

Parking (Coach/Bus): South Common

Police Force and Tel No: Lincolnshire (01522 529911)

Disabled Visitors' Facilities
  Wheelchairs: South Park Stand
  Blind: No special facility

KEY

C Club Offices

S Club Shop

E Entrance(s) for visiting supporters

R Refreshment bars for visiting supporters

T Toilets for visiting supporters

⬆ North direction (approx)

❶ A46 High Street
❷ Sincil Bank
❸ Sausthorpe Street
❹ Cross Street
❺ A158 Canwick Road
❻ A158 South Park Avenue
❼ Car Park
❽ Lincoln Central BR Station (½ mile)

Left: Vastly experienced Trevor Hebberd pictured here in City's change strip during October 1994.

LIVERPOOL

Anfield Road, Liverpool, L4 0TH

Tel No: 0151 263 2361
Advance Tickets Tel No: 0151 260 8680
League: F.A. Premier
Brief History: Founded 1892. Anfield Ground formerly Everton F.C. Ground. Joined Football League in 1893. Record attendance 61,905.
(Total) Current Capacity: Approx 41,000 (all seated)
Visiting Supporters' Allocation: 3,120
Club Colours: Red shirts, red shorts
Nearest Railway Station: Kirkdale

Parking (Car): Stanley car park
Parking (Coach/Bus): Priory Road & Pinehurst Avenue
Police Force and Tel No: Merseyside (0151 709 6010)
Disabled Visitors' Facilities
  Wheelchairs: Lothair Road
  Blind: Commentary available
Anticipated Development(s): Additional work to increase capacity to approx 44,000 in 1996.

KEY
C Club Offices
S Club Shop
E Entrance(s) for visiting supporters

↑ North direction (approx)

❶ Car Park
❷ Anfield Road
❸ A5089 Walton Breck Road
❹ Kemlyn Road
❺ Kirkdale BR Station (1 mile)
❻ Utting Avenue
❼ Stanley Park
❽ Spion Kop

Right: Shortly to become a regular in the England set-up, Jamie Redknapp possesses all of the qualities usually found in the Anfield engine room.

LUTON TOWN

Kenilworth Road Stadium, 1 Maple Road, Luton, LU4 8AW

Tel No: 01582 411622
Advance Tickets Tel No: 01582 30748
League: 1st Division
Brief History: Founded 1885 from an amalgamation of Wanderers F.C. & Excelsior F.C. Former Grounds: Dallow Lane & Dunstable Road, moved to Kenilworth Road in 1905. Record attendance 30,069.
(Total) Current Capacity: 11,099
Club Colours: White shirts with royal blue & orange stripe on collar & waist. Royal blue shorts with white & orange trim.

Nearest Railway Station: Luton

Parking (Car): Street parking

Parking (Coach/Bus): Luton bus station

Police Force and Tel No: Bedfordshire (01582 401212)

Disabled Visitors' Facilities
　Wheelchairs: Kenilworth Road
　Blind: Commentary available

KEY

C Club Offices
S Club Shop
E Entrance(s) for visiting supporters
R Refreshment bars for visiting supporters
T Toilets for visiting supporters

↑ North direction (approx)

❶ To M1 Junction 11
❷ Wimborne Road
❸ Kenilworth Road
❹ Oak Road
❺ Dunstable Road
❻ Luton BR Station (1 mile)
❼ Ticket Office

Left: A superb servant during his days with the Hatters, Trevor Peake continues to excel at the heart of Luton defence.

MANCHESTER CITY

Maine Road, Moss Side, Manchester, M14 7WN

Tel No: 0161 226 1191

Advance Tickets Tel No: 0161 226 2224

League: F.A. Premier

Brief History: Founded 1880 as West Gorton, changed name to Ardwick (reformed 1887) and to Manchester City in 1894. Former grounds: Clowes Street, Kirkmanshulme Cricket Club, Donkey Common, Pink Bank Lane & Hyde Road, moved to Maine Road in 1923. Founder-members 2nd Division (1892). Record attendance 84,569 (record for Football League ground).

(Total) Current Capacity: 32,500 (all seated)

Club Colours: Sky blue shirts, white shorts

Nearest Railway Station: Manchester Piccadilly (2½ miles)

Parking (Car): Street parking & local schools

Parking (Coach/Bus): Kippax Street car park

Police Force and Tel No: Greater Manchester (0161 872 5050)

Disabled Visitors' Facilities
  Wheelchairs: Umbro Stand / Kippax Stand
  Blind: Main Stand 'G' Block

KEY

C Club Offices

S Club Shop

E Entrance(s) for visiting supporters

↑ North direction (approx)

❶ Thornton Road
❷ South Upper Lloyd Street
❸ To A5103 Princess Road
❹ To City Centre and Manchester Piccadilly BR Station (2½ miles)
❺ To A6010 & M31 Junction 7
❻ Maine Road

Left: Maine Road fans will tell you that this is the German buy of the decade and not a certain short term Tottenham player! Uwe Rossler is now a firm favourite at Manchester City.

MANCHESTER UNITED

Old Trafford, Warwick Road North, Manchester, M16 0RA

Tel No: 0161 872 1661
Advance Tickets Tel No: 0161 872 0199
League: F.A. Premier
Brief History: Founded in 1878 as 'Newton Heath L & Y', later Newton Heath, changed to Manchester United in 1902. Former Grounds: North Road, Monsall & Bank Street, Clayton, moved to Old Trafford in 1910 (used Manchester City F.C. Ground 1941-49). Founder-members Second Division (1892). Record attendance 76,962.
(Total) Current Capacity: 43,500 (all seated). Temporarily limited to approx 31,000 during rebuilding in 1995/96 season.

Club Colours: Red shirts, white shorts
Nearest Railway Station: At Ground
Parking (Car): Lancashire Cricket Ground & White City
Parking (Coach/Bus): As directed by Police
Police Force and Tel No: Greater Manchester (0161 872 5050)
Disabled Visitors' Facilities
  Wheelchairs: In front of Main Stand.
  Blind: Commentary available
Anticipated Development(s): On completion of the 1995/96 season total capacity will be increased to approx 55,000 by rebuilding the North Stand.

KEY

C Club Offices
S Club Shop

↑ North direction (approx)

❶ A5081 Trafford Park Road to M63 Junction 4 (5 miles)
❷ A56 Chester Road
❸ Manchester Ship Canal
❹ Old Trafford Cricket Ground
❺ To Parking and Warwick Road BR Station

Right: Eric Cantona fends off Ipswich's Linighan in September 1994. However, the United star's fiery temperament ensured that he didn't finish the season on the pitch.

MANSFIELD TOWN

Field Mill Ground, Quarry Lane, Mansfield, Notts

Tel No: 01623 23567
Advance Tickets Tel No: 01623 23567
League: 3rd Division
Brief History: Founded 1910 as Mansfield
Wesleyans Boys Brigade, changed to Mansfield
Town in 1914. Former Grounds: Pelham
Street, Newgate Lane & The Prairie, moved to
Field Mill in 1919. Record attendance 24,467.
(Total) Current Capacity: 10,315 (3,448
seated)
Club Colours: Amber with blue trim shirts,
Amber shorts with blue trim.

Nearest Railway Station: Mansfield Alfreton
Parkway (9 miles)
Parking (Car): Car park at Ground
Parking (Coach/Bus): Car park at Ground
Police Force and Tel No: Nottinghamshire
(01623 420999)
Disabled Visitors' Facilities
Wheelchairs: Bishop Street
(Entrance at North end of West stand)
Blind: No special facility

KEY

C Club Offices
E Entrance(s) for visiting
supporters

↑ North direction (approx)

❶ Car Park
❷ Quarry Lane
❸ A60 Nottingham Road to M1
Junction 27
❹ Portland Street
❺ To A38 and M1 Junction 28
❻ Town Centre

Left: Town's Paul Holland (in striped shirt) holds off the attentions of Chesterfield's Nicky Law in this Third Division promotion Play-Off match.

MIDDLESBROUGH

The Cellnet Riverside Stadium, Middlesbrough, Cleveland

Tel No: 01642 227227

League: FA Premier

Brief History: Founded 1876. Former Grounds: Archery Ground (Albert Park), Breckon Hill Road, Linthorpe Road, moved to Ayresome Park in 1903, and to current ground in Summer 1995. FA Amateur Cup winners 1894 and 1897 (joined Football League in 1899). Record attendance (Ayresome Park) 53,596.

(Total) Current Capacity: Approx. 30,000 (all seated)

Club Colours: Red shirts with white yoke, white shorts

Nearest Railway Station: Middlesbrough

Parking (Car): Information not confirmed at time of writing

Parking (Coach/Bus): Information not confirmed at time of writing

Police Force and Tel No: Cleveland (01642 248184)

Disabled Visitors' Facilities

Wheelchairs: Information not confirmed at time of writing

Blind: Information not confirmed at time of writing

KEY

⬆ North direction (approx)

❶ Cargo Fleet Road
❷ To A66 and Middlesbrough
   BR station (¹/2 mile)
❸ To Town Centres
❹ Middlesbrough Docks
   (1 mile) and Town Centre

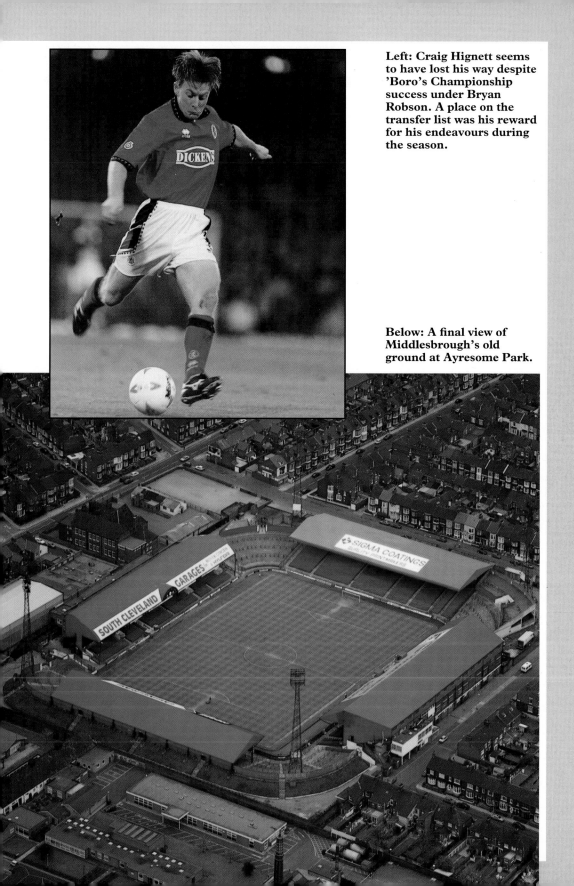

Left: Craig Hignett seems to have lost his way despite 'Boro's Championship success under Bryan Robson. A place on the transfer list was his reward for his endeavours during the season.

Below: A final view of Middlesbrough's old ground at Ayresome Park.

MILLWALL

New Den, Bolina Road, London, SE16

Tel No: 0171 232 1222
Advance Tickets Tel No: 0171 231 9999
League: 1st Division
Brief History: Founded 1885 as Millwall Rovers, changed name to Millwall Athletic (1889) and Millwall (1925). Former Grounds: Glengall Road, East Ferry Road (2 separate Grounds), North Greenwich Ground and The Den - Cold Blow Lane - moved to New Den 1993/94 season. Founder-members Third Division (1920). Record attendance (at The Den) 48,672.

(Total) Current Capacity: 20,150 (20,150 seated)
Club Colours: Blue shirts, Blue shorts
Nearest Railway Station: South Bermondsey or Surrey Docks (tube)
Parking (Car): Juno Way car parking (8 mins. walk)
Parking (Coach/Bus): At Ground
Police Force and Tel No: Metropolitan (0171 679 9217)
Disabled Visitors' Facilities
    Wheelchairs: Area allocated
    Blind: Commentary available

KEY

C Club Offices
S Club Shop
E Entrance(s) for visiting supporters

↑ North direction (approx)

❶ Bolina Road
❷ South Bermondsey BR
❸ Surrey Quays Underground
❹ Rotherhithe Tunnel
❺ Ilderton Road
❻ The 'Old' Den
❼ River Thames

Left: Without doubt a star of the future, Millwall left back Ben Thatcher points the way for his Lions colleagues.

NEWCASTLE UNITED

St. James' Park, Newcastle-upon-Tyne, NE1 4ST

Tel No: 0191 232 8361

Advance Tickets Tel No: 0191 261 1571

League: F. A. Premier

Brief History: Founded in 1882 as Newcastle East End, changed to Newcastle United in 1892. Former Grounds: Chillingham Road, moved to St. James' Park (former home of defunct Newcastle West End) in 1892. Record attendance 68,386.

(Total) Current Capacity: 35,642 (all seated)

Club Colours: Black & white striped shirts, black shorts

Nearest Railway Station: Newcastle Central

Parking (Car): Leazes car park & street parking

Parking (Coach/Bus): Leazes car park

Police Force and Tel No: Northumbria (0191 232 3451)

Disabled Visitors' Facilities
  Wheelchairs: Sir John Hall Stand
  Blind: Commentary available

KEY

C Club Offices
E Entrance(s) for visiting supporters
S Club Shop

↑ North direction (approx)

❶ St. James' Street
❷ Strawberry Place
❸ Gallowgate
❹ Wellington Street
❺ To Newcastle Central BR Station (1/2 mile) & A6127 (M)
❻ Car Park

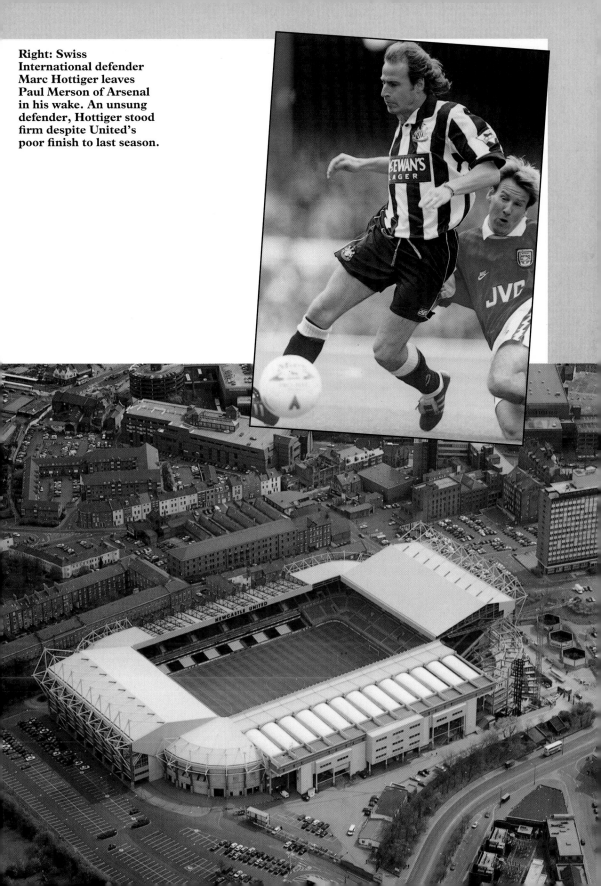

Right: Swiss International defender Marc Hottiger leaves Paul Merson of Arsenal in his wake. An unsung defender, Hottiger stood firm despite United's poor finish to last season.

NORTHAMPTON TOWN

Sixfields Stadium, Northampton, NN5 4EG

Tel No: 01604 757773

League: 3rd Division

Brief History: Founded 1897. Former, County, Ground was part of Northamptonshire County Cricket Ground. Moved to Sixfields Stadium during early 1994/95 season. Record attendance 24,523 (at County Ground)

(Total) Current Capacity: 7,653 (all seated)

Visiting Supporters' Allocation: 962 (all seated)

Club Colours: White with claret trim shirts, white with claret trim shorts

Nearest Railway Station: Northampton Castle

Parking (Car): Adjacent to Ground

Parking (Coach/Bus): Adjacent to Ground

Police Force and Tel No: Northants (01604 33221)

Disabled Visitors' Facilities
   Wheelchairs: Available on all four sides.
   Blind: Available.

KEY

- **C** Club Offices
- **S** Club Shop
- **E** Entrance(s) for visiting supporters
- **R** Refreshment bars for visiting supporters
- **T** Toilets for visiting supporters

↑ North direction (approx)

❶ Weedon Road to Town Centre and Northampton Castle BR station (two miles)
❷ Upton Way, to M1 Junction 15A
❸ A45, to M1 Junction 16
❹ Car parks

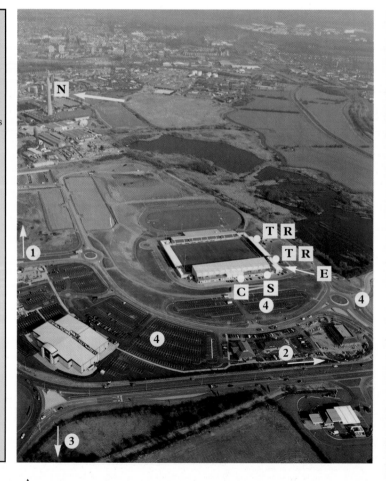

Right: Ian Simpson pictured in action during the first match at the new Sixfields Stadium, when Barnet were the Cobblers' Third Division opponents.

NORWICH CITY

Carrow Road, Norwich, NR1 1JE

Tel No: 01603 760760
Advance Tickets Tel No: 01603 761661
League: 1st Division
Brief History: Founded 1902. Former grounds: Newmarket Road and the Nest, Rosary Road; moved to Carrow Road in 1935. Founder members 3rd Division (1920). Record attendance 43,984.
(Total) Current Capacity: 21,260 (seated)

Club Colours: Yellow shirts, green shorts
Nearest Railway Station: Norwich
Parking (Car): City centre car parks
Parking (Coach/Bus): Lower Clarence Road
Police Force and Tel No: Norfolk (01603 621212)
Disabled Visitors' Facilities
   Wheelchairs: South Stand (heated)
   Blind: No special facility

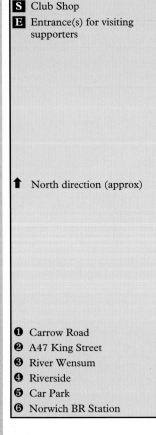

KEY
C Club Offices
S Club Shop
E Entrance(s) for visiting supporters

⬆ North direction (approx)

❶ Carrow Road
❷ A47 King Street
❸ River Wensum
❹ Riverside
❺ Car Park
❻ Norwich BR Station

Left: Some Premiership fans have still to come to terms with Norwich's relegation at the end of the 1994/95 season. Despite the efforts of former Leeds defender Jon Newsome, City must rebuild in Division One.

NOTTINGHAM FOREST

City Ground, Nottingham, NG2 5FJ

Tel No: 0115 952 6000
Advance Tickets Tel No: 0115 952 6002
League: F.A. Premier
Brief History: Founded 1865 as Forest Football
Club, changed name to Nottingham Forest
(c.1879). Former Grounds: Forest Recreation
Ground, Meadow Cricket Ground, Trent
Bridge (Cricket Ground), Parkside, Gregory
Ground & Town Ground, moved to City
Ground in 1898. Founder-members of Second
Division (1892). Record attendance 49,045.

(Total) Current capacity: 30,500 (all seated)
Visiting Supporters' Allocation: Approx 4,000
Club Colours: Red shirts, white shorts
Nearest Railway Station: Nottingham Midland
Parking (Car): East car park & street parking
Parking (Coach/Bus): East car park
Police Force and Tel No: Nottinghamshire
(0115 948 1888)
Disabled Visitors' Facilities
  Wheelchairs: Front of Executive Stand
  Blind: No special facility

KEY

C Club Offices
S Club Shop
E Entrance(s) for visiting
supporters

↑ North direction (approx)

❶ Radcliffe Road
❷ Lady Bay Bridge Road
❸ Trent Bridge
❹ Trent Bridge Cricket Ground
❺ Notts County F.C.
❻ River Trent
❼ Nottingham Midland BR
Station (1/2 mile)

Left: Steve Stone bears down Forest's right flank. He is, perhaps, one of the Premiership's most under-rated players and may well be destined for International recognition soon.

NOTTS COUNTY

Meadow Lane, Nottingham, NG2 3HJ

Tel No: 0115 952 9000

Advance Tickets Tel No: 0115 952 7210

League: 2nd Division

Brief History: Founded 1862 (oldest club in Football League) as Nottingham, changed to Notts County in c.1882. Former Grounds: Notts Cricket Ground (Beeston), Castle Cricket Ground, Trent Bridge Cricket Ground, moved to Meadow Lane in 1910. Founder-members Football League (1888). Record attendance 47,310.

(Total) Current Capacity: 20,380 (seated)

Visiting Supporters' Allocation: 5,438 (seated)

Club Colours: Black & white stripes, amber sleeves & trim shirts, white shorts.

Nearest Railway Station: Nottingham Midland

Parking (Car): Mainly street parking

Parking (Coach/Bus): Cattle market

Police Force and Tel No: Nottingham (0115 948 1888)

Disabled Visitors' Facilities
  Wheelchairs: Meadow Lane/Jimmy Sirrel/Derek Pavis Stands.
  Blind: No special facility

KEY

C Club Offices
S Club Shop
E Entrance(s) for visiting supporters
R Refreshment bars for visiting supporters
T Toilets for visiting supporters

↑ North direction (approx)

❶ A6011 Meadow Lane
❷ County Road
❸ A60 London Road
❹ River Trent
❺ Nottingham Midland BR Station (¹/2 mile)

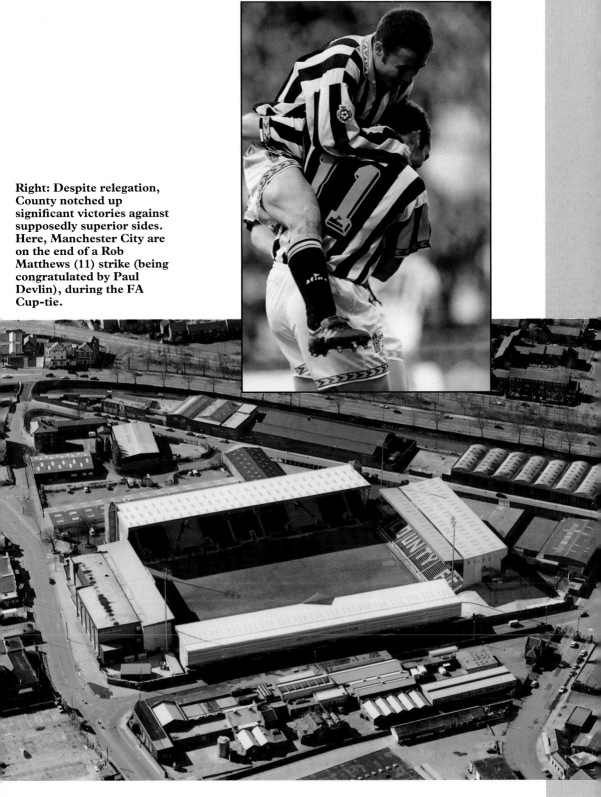

Right: Despite relegation, County notched up significant victories against supposedly superior sides. Here, Manchester City are on the end of a Rob Matthews (11) strike (being congratulated by Paul Devlin), during the FA Cup-tie.

OLDHAM ATHLETIC

Boundary Park, Oldham, OL1 2PA

Tel No: 0161 624 4972
Advance Tickets Tel No: 0161 624 4972
League: 1st Division
Brief History: Founded 1897 as Pine Villa, changed name to Oldham Athletic in 1899. Former Grounds: Berry's Field, Pine Mill, Athletic Ground (later named Boundary Park), Hudson Fold, moved to Boundary Park in 1906. Record attendance 47,671.
(Total) Current Capacity: 13,500 (all seated)
Visiting Supporters' Allocation: 1,500 minimum, 5,000 maximum

Club Colours: Blue shirts, blue shorts

Nearest Railway Station: Oldham Werneth

Parking (Car): Lookers Stand car park

Parking (Coach/Bus): At Ground

Police Force and Tel No: Greater Manchester (0161 624 0444)

Disabled Visitors' Facilities
   Wheelchairs: Lookers Stand
   Blind: Commentary available

KEY

C Club Offices
E Entrance(s) for visiting supporters

↑ North direction (approx)

❶ A663 Broadway
❷ Furtherwood Road
❸ Chadderton Way
❹ To A627(M) and M62
❺ To Oldham Werneth BR Station (1½ miles)
❻ Car Park

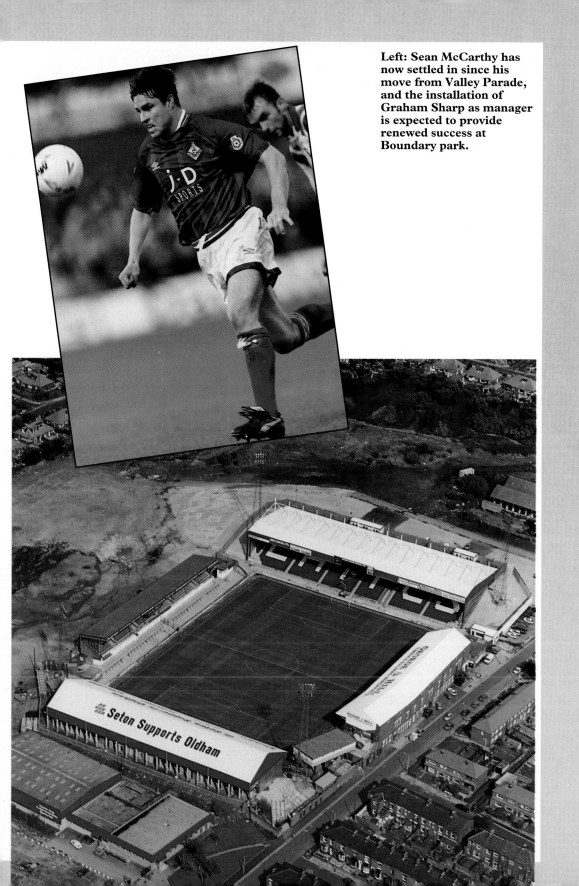

Left: Sean McCarthy has now settled in since his move from Valley Parade, and the installation of Graham Sharp as manager is expected to provide renewed success at Boundary park.

OXFORD UNITED

Manor Ground, London Road, Headington, Oxford, OX3 7RS

Tel No: 01865 61503
Advance Tickets Tel No: 01865 61503
League: 2nd Division
Brief History: Founded 1893 as Headington (later Headington United), changed name to Oxford United in 1960. Former grounds: Brittania Inn Field, Headington Quarry, Wooten's Field, Manor Ground, The Paddocks, moved back to Manor Ground in 1925. Record attendance 22,730.
(Total) Current Capacity: 11,071 (2,777 seated)
Club Colours: Yellow with navy trim shirts, navy with yellow trim shorts.

Nearest Railway Station: Oxford (3 miles)

Parking (Car): Street parking

Parking (Coach/Bus): Headley Way

Police Force and Tel No: Thames Valley (01865 777501)

Disabled Visitors' Facilities
  Wheelchairs: Beech Road
  Blind: No special facility

Anticipated Development(s): Anticipated move to new 15,000 capacity all-seated stadium.

KEY
C Club Offices
E Entrance(s) for visiting supporters
R Refreshment bars for visiting supporters

↑ North direction (approx)

❶ A420 London Road
❷ Osler Road
❸ To City Centre and Oxford BR Station (3 miles)
❹ To A40 and Ring Road (¾ mile)
❺ Cuckoo Lane

**Right: United favourite
Chris Allen is pictured in a
September 1994 League
encounter at the Manor
Ground. Together with
Moody and Rush, Allen
proved a handful for many
Division Two defences.**

PETERBOROUGH UNITED

London Road, Peterborough, Cambs, PE2 8AL

Tel No: 01733 63947
Advance Tickets Tel No: 01733 63947
League: 2nd Division
Brief History: Founded in 1934, (no connection with former 'Peterborough and Fletton United' FC). Elected to Football League in 1960. Record attendance 30,096.
(Total) Current Capacity: 18,978 (4,715 seated)

Club Colours: Blue shirts, white shorts
Nearest Railway Station: Peterborough
Parking (Car): At ground
Parking (Coach/Bus): At ground
Police Force and Tel No: Cambridgeshire (01733 63232)
Disabled Visitors' Facilities
  Wheelchairs: London Road End
  Blind: No special facility

KEY

C Club Offices
S Club Shop
E Entrance(s) for visiting supporters
R Refreshment bars for visiting supporters
T Toilets for visiting supporters

⬆ North direction (approx)

❶ A15 London Road
❷ Car Parks
❸ Peterborough BR Station (1 mile)
❹ Glebe Road
❺ A605
❻ To A1 (5 miles)

Right: Peterborough defender Liburd Henry enjoys the upper hand in this Posh (change strip) League encounter with Birmingham City at St Andrews.

PLYMOUTH ARGYLE

Home Park, Plymouth, PL2 3DQ

Tel No: 01752 562561

Advance Tickets Tel No: 01752 562561

League: 3rd Division

Brief History: Founded 1886 as Argyle Athletic Club, changed name to Plymouth Argyle in 1903. Founder-members Third Division (1920). Record attendance 43,596

(Total) Current Capacity: 19,900 (6,700 seated)

Club Colours: Green & white striped shirts, black shorts

Nearest Railway Station: Plymouth

Parking (Car): Car park adjacent

Parking (Coach/Bus): Central car park

Police Force and Tel No: Devon & Cornwall (01752 701188)

Disabled Visitors' Facilities
Wheelchairs: Devonport End
Blind: Commentary available

KEY

C Club Offices

S Club Shop

E Entrance(s) for visiting supporters

R Refreshment bars for visiting supporters

T Toilets for visiting supporters

↑ North direction (approx)

❶ Outland Road
❷ Car Park
❸ Devonport Road
❹ Central Park
❺ Town Centre & Plymouth BR Station (¾ mile)

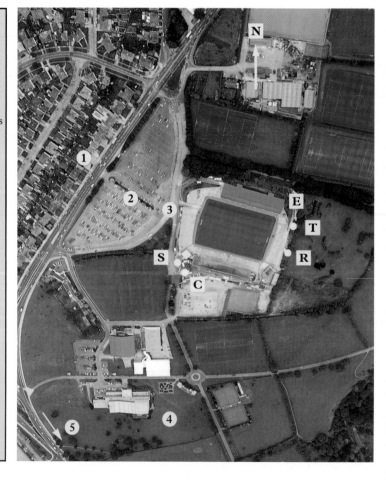

126

Left: Former Carlisle and Derby County full-back Mark Patterson is about to hurl the ball towards his forwards during this pre-season friendly at Home Park.

PORTSMOUTH

Fratton Park, 57 Frogmore Road, Portsmouth, Hants, PO4 8RA

Tel No: 01705 731204
Advance Tickets Tel No: 01705 750825
League: 1st Division
Brief History: Founded 1898. Founder-members Third Division (1920). Record attendance 51,385.
(Total) Current Capacity: 26,452 (6,652 seated)
Visiting Supporters' Allocation: 5,848 (1,228 seated)
Club Colours: Blue shirts, white shorts

Nearest Railway Station: Fratton
Parking (Car): Street parking
Parking (Coach/Bus): As directed by Police
Police Force and Tel No: Hampshire (01705 321111)
Disabled Visitors' Facilities
 Wheelchairs: Frogmore Road
 Blind: No special facility
Anticipated Development(s): (Editor's note: Update information regarding Ground not advised.)

KEY

C	Club Offices
S	Club Shop
E	Entrance(s) for visiting supporters
R	Refreshment bars for visiting supporters
T	Toilets for visiting supporters

↑ North direction (approx)

❶ Alverstone Road
❷ Carisbrook Road
❸ A288 Milton Road
❹ A2030 Eastern Road to A27
❺ A2030 Goldsmith Avenue
❻ Fratton BR Station (½ mile)

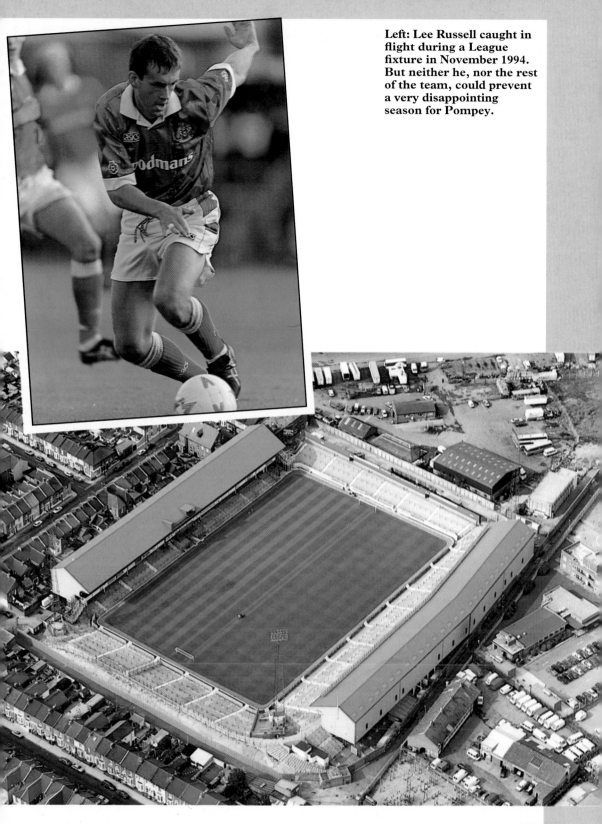

**Left: Lee Russell caught in
flight during a League
fixture in November 1994.
But neither he, nor the rest
of the team, could prevent
a very disappointing
season for Pompey.**

PORT VALE

Vale Park, Burslem, Stoke-on-Trent, ST6 1AW

Tel No: 01782 814134

Advance Tickets Tel No: 01782 814134

League: 1st Division

Brief History: Founded 1876 as Burslem Port Vale, changed name to 'Port Vale' in 1907 (reformed club). Former Grounds: The Meadows Longport, Moorland Road Athletic Ground, Cobridge Athletic Grounds, Recreation Ground Hanley, moved to Vale Park in 1950. Founder-members Second Division (1892). Record attendance 50,000.

(Total) Current Capacity: 23,589 (12,442 seated)

Club Colours: White shirts, black shorts

Nearest Railway Station: Stoke

Parking (Car): Car park at Ground

Parking (Coach/Bus): Hamil Road car park

Police Force and Tel No: Staffordshire (01782 577114)

Disabled Visitors' Facilities

Wheelchairs: Specialist Stand - Lorne Street

Blind: Commentary available

KEY

C Club Offices

E Entrance(s) for visiting supporters

↑ North direction (approx)

❶ Car Parks
❷ Hamil Road
❸ Lorne Street
❹ B5051 Moorland Road

Left: Tony Naylor puts his best foot forward during this League encounter at Vale Park in mid-January 1995.

PRESTON NORTH END

Lowthorpe Road, Deepdale, PR1 6RU

Tel No: 01772 795919
Advance Tickets Tel No: 01772 795919
League: 3rd Division
Brief History: Founded 1867 as a Rugby Club, changed to soccer in 1881. Former ground: Moor park, moved to (later named) Deepdale in 1875. Founder-members Football League (1888). Record attendance 42,684.
(Total) Current Capacity: 16,500 (3,000 seated)
Club Colours: White shirts, blue shorts

Nearest Railway Station: Preston (2 miles)
Parking (Car): West Stand car park
Parking (Coach/Bus): West Stand car park
Police Force and Tel No: Lancashire (01772 203203)
Disabled Visitors' Facilities
  Wheelchairs: Deepdale Road
  Blind: Earphones Commentary
Anticipated Development(s): (Editor's note: Update information regarding Ground not advised.)

KEY

C Club Offices
S Club Shop
E Entrance(s) for visiting supporters
R Refreshment bars for visiting supporters
T Toilets for visiting supporters

⬆ North direction (approx)

❶ A6033 Deepdale Road
❷ Lawthorpe Road
❸ Car Park
❹ A5085 Blackpool Road
❺ Preston BR Station (2 miles)
❻ Fulwood End – Spion Kop

132

Left: Preston's Raymond Sharp is caught in 'The Lilywhites' third strip on 13 December 1994. For the 1995/96 season, Preston will see a new sponsor's name on their shirts – Baxi.

QUEENS PARK RANGERS

Rangers Stadium, South Africa Road, London, W12 7PA

Tel No: 0181 743 0262

Tickets and Info. Tel No: 0181 749 5744

League: F.A. Premier

Brief History: Founded 1885 as 'St. Jude's Institute', amalgamated with Christchurch Rangers to become Queens Park Rangers in 1886. Football League record number of former Grounds and Ground moves (13 different venues, 17 changes), including White City Stadium (twice) final move to Rangers Stadium (then named Loftus Road) in 1963. Founder-members Third Division (1920). Record attendance 35,353.

(Total) Current Capacity: 19,500 (all seated)

Club Colours: Blue & white hooped shirts, white shorts

Nearest Railway Station: Shepherds Bush and White City (both tube)

Parking (Car): White City NCP & street parking

Parking (Coach/Bus): White City NCP

Police Force and Tel No: Metropolitan (0181 246 2725)

Disabled Visitors' Facilities

  Wheelchairs: Ellerslie Road Stand & West Paddock

  Blind: Ellerslie Road Stand

KEY

C Club Offices

S Club Shop

E Entrance(s) for visiting supporters

↑ North direction (approx)

❶ South Africa Road

❷ To White City Tube Station, A219 Wood Lane and A40 Western Avenue

❸ A4020 Uxbridge Road

❹ To Shepherds Bush Tube Station

❺ Ellerslie Road

Left: Diminutive ex-Bristol Rovers winger, Andrew Impey, controls the ball in a March 1995 Premiership encounter at Loftus Road.

READING

Elm Park, Norfolk Road, Reading, RG3 2EF

Tel No: 01734 507878
Advance Tickets Tel No: 01734 507878
League: 1st Division
Brief History: Founded 1871. (Amalgamated with Reading Hornets in 1877 and with Earley in 1889). Former Grounds: Reading Recreation Ground, Reading Cricket Ground, Coley Park and Caversham Cricket Ground, moved to Elm Park in 1895. Founder-members Third Division (1920). Record attendance 33,042.
(Total) Current Capacity: 14,058 (2,242 seated)
Visiting Supporters' Allocation: 3,174 (342 seated)

Club Colours: White with blue hoops shirts, white shorts
Nearest Railway Station: Reading West
Parking (Car): Street parking & Park & Ride scheme from Prospect School, Honey End Lane.
Parking (Coach/Bus): The Meadway
Police Force and Tel No: Thames Valley (01734 536000)
Disabled Visitors' Facilities
  Wheelchairs: Norfolk Road
  Blind: Organised by Hospital Radio

KEY

C Club Offices
S Club Shop
E Entrance(s) for visiting supporters
R Refreshment bars for visiting supporters
T Toilets for visiting supporters

↑ North direction (approx)

❶ Tilehurst Road
❷ Norfolk Road
❸ County Cricket Ground
❹ Reading West BR Station (½ mile)
❺ Liebenrood Road to A4 Bath Road (¼ mile)

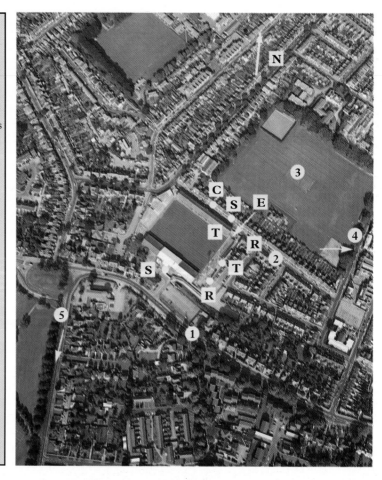

Left: Out for a long spell last year, Adrian Williams returned to bolster the Royals' end of season push for promotion. Sadly, a Welsh cap could not compensate for losing to Bolton in the Wembley Play-Off final.

137

ROCHDALE

Willbutts Lane, Spotland, Rochdale, OL11 5DS

Tel No: 01706 44648
Advance Tickets Tel No: 01706 44648
League: 3rd Division
Brief History: Founded 1907 from former Rochdale Town F.C. (founded 1900). Founder-members Third Division North (1921). Record attendance 24,231.
(Total) Current Capacity: 9,000 (2,000 seated)
Visiting Supporters' Allocation: 1,500 (250 seated)

Club Colours: Blue & white shirts, blue shorts
Nearest Railway Station: Rochdale
Parking (Car): Rear of ground
Parking (Coach/Bus): Rear of ground
Police Force and Tel No: Greater Manchester (01706 47401)
Disabled Visitors' Facilities
  Wheelchairs: Main stand - disabled area
  Blind: No special facility

KEY

C Club Offices
S Club Shop
E Entrance(s) for visiting supporters
R Refreshment bars for visiting supporters
T Toilets for visiting supporters

⬆ North direction (approx)

❶ Willbutts Lane
❷ A627 Edenfield Road
❸ Rochdale BR Station (1/2 mile)
❹ Sandy Lane

138

Left: The home team's Andy Thackeray is pictured during the League Division Three encounter with Lincoln City on 30 August 1994.

ROTHERHAM UNITED

Millmoor Ground, Rotherham, S60 1HR

Tel No: 01709 562434
Advance Tickets Tel No: 01709 562434
League: 2nd Division
Brief History: Founded 1877 (as Thornhill, later Thornhill United), changed name to Rotherham County in 1905 and to Rotherham United in 1925, (amalgamated with Rotherham Town - Football League members 1893-97 - in 1925). Former Grounds include: Red House Ground & Clifton Lane Cricket Ground, moved to Millmoor in 1907. Record attendance 25,000.
(Total) Current Capacity: 11,533 (4,486 seated)

Visiting Supporters' Allocation: 4,000 (1,000 seated)
Club Colours: Red shirts, white shorts
Nearest Railway Station: Rotherham Central
Parking (Car): Kimberworth and Main Street car parks, plus large car park adjacent to ground.
Parking (Coach/Bus): As directed by Police
Police Force and Tel No: South Yorkshire (01709 371121)
Disabled Visitors' Facilities
  Wheelchairs: Millmoor Lane
  Blind: No special facility

KEY

C Club Offices
S Club Shop
E Entrance(s) for visiting supporters
R Refreshment bars for visiting supporters
T Toilets for visiting supporters

↑ North direction (approx)

❶ Car Park
❷ Rotherham Central BR Station
❸ A6109 Masborough Road
❹ Millmoor Lane
❺ To A6178 and M1 Junction 34

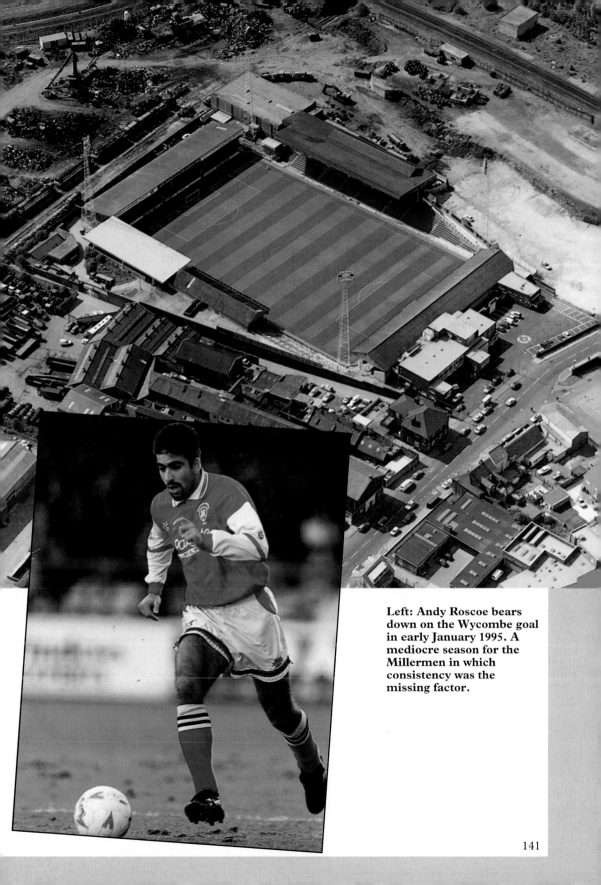

Left: Andy Roscoe bears
down on the Wycombe goal
in early January 1995. A
mediocre season for the
Millermen in which
consistency was the
missing factor.

SCARBOROUGH

McCain Stadium, Seamer Road, Scarborough, N. Yorkshire YO12 4HF

Tel No: 01723 375094
Advance Tickets Tel No: 01723 375094
League: 3rd Division
Brief History: Founded 1879 as 'Scarborough Cricketers F.C.' changed name to 'Scarborough F.C.' in 1887. Former grounds: North Marine (Cricket) Ground and Recreation Ground, moved to (then named) Athletic Ground in 1898. Promoted to Football League in 1987. Record attendance 11,124.
(Total) Current Capacity: 6,832 (2,149 seated)
Visiting Supporters' Allocation: 2,656 (288 seated)

Club Colours: Red shirts, white shorts
Nearest Railway Station: Scarborough Central (2 miles)
Parking (Car): Street parking
Parking (Coach/Bus): Weaponess coach/car park
Police Force and Tel No: North Yorkshire (01723 500300)
Disabled Visitors' Facilities
   Wheelchairs: Main Stand, Edgehill Road end.
   Blind: No special facility

KEY

C Club Offices
E Entrance(s) for visiting supporters
R Refreshment bars for visiting supporters
T Toilets for visiting supporters

⬆ North direction (approx)

❶ A64 Seamer Road
❷ Scarborough Central BR Station (2 miles)
❸ To York
❹ McCain Stand

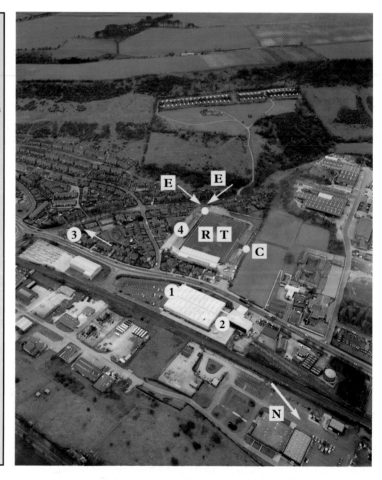

Left: Scarborough's Ian Ironside and Scunthorpe's Michael Walsh battle it out in the Boro' goal during this League Division 3 fixture on 22 April 1995.

SCUNTHORPE UNITED

Glanford Park, Doncaster Road, Scunthorpe DN15 8TD

Tel No: 01724 848077
Advance Tickets Tel No: 01724 848077
League: 3rd Division
Brief History: Founded 1899 as Scunthorpe United, amalgamated with North Lindsey to become 'Scunthorpe & Lindsey United in 1912. Changed name to Scunthorpe United in 1956. Former grounds: Crosby (Lindsey United) & Old Showground, moved to Glanford Park in 1988. Elected to Football League in 1950. Record attendance 8,775 (23,935 at Old Showground).

(Total) Current Capacity: 9,200 (6,400 seated)
Club Colours: Sky blue shirts with two claret rings on sleeves, white shorts with claret stripe.
Nearest Railway Station: Scunthorpe
Parking (Car): At ground
Parking (Coach/Bus): At ground
Police Force and Tel No: Humberside (01724 282888)
Disabled Visitors' Facilities
 Wheelchairs: Clugston Stand
 Blind: Commentary available

KEY

C Club Offices
S Club Shop
E Entrance(s) for visiting supporters
R Refreshment bars for visiting supporters
T Toilets for visiting supporters

↑ North direction (approx)

❶ Car Park
❷ Glanford Stand
❸ A18 Scunthorpe BR Station and Town Centre (1½ miles)
❹ M181 and M180 Junction 3

Left: Mark Smith seen in United's colours during the 1994/95 season. Perhaps the venue suggested by the sponsor's logo would be a more desirable location after a mediocre campaign for Scunthorpe!

SHEFFIELD UNITED

Bramall Lane, Sheffield, S2 4SU

Tel No: 0114 273 8955
Advance Tickets Tel No: 0114 276 6771
League: 1st Division
Brief History: Founded 1889. (Sheffield Wednesday occasionally used Bramall Lane c.1880). Founder-members 2nd Division (1892). Record attendance 68,287
(Total) Current Capacity: 23,390 (all seated)
Visiting Supporters' Allocation: 2,560 (seated)
Club Colours: Red & white striped shirts, black shorts

Nearest Railway Station: Sheffield Midland
Parking (Car): Street parking
Parking (Coach/Bus): As directed by Police
Police Force and Tel No: South Yorkshire (0114 276 8522)
Disabled Visitors' Facilities
  Wheelchairs: (Temporary) South Stand
  Blind: Commentary available
Anticipated Development(s): (Editor's note: John Street Stand to be rebuilt summer 1995. Detailed update not advised.)

KEY
C Club Offices
E Entrance(s) for visiting supporters
R Refreshment bars for visiting supporters
T Toilets for visiting supporters

↑ North direction (approx)

❶ A621 Bramall Lane
❷ Shoreham Street
❸ Car Park
❹ Sheffield Midland BR Station (¼ mile)
❺ John Street
❻ Spion Kop

Left: Jostein Flo, with suitable pleasure on his face, has just scored for United against Oldham. This was the Blades second goal against the Latics, during the October 1994 League encounter.

SHEFFIELD WEDNESDAY

Hillsborough, Sheffield, S6 1SW

Tel No: 0114 234 3122
Advance Tickets Tel No: 0114 233 7233
League: F.A. Premier
Brief History: Founded 1867 as The Wednesday F.C. (changed to Sheffield Wednesday c.1930). Former Grounds: London Road, Wyrtle Road (Heeley), Sheaf House Ground, Encliffe & Olive Grove (Bramall Lane also used occasionally), moved to Hillsborough (then named 'Owlerton' in 1899). Founder-members Second Division (1892). Record attendance 72,841.
(Total) Current Capacity: 36,020 (all seated)
Visiting Supporters' Allocation: 4,183 (all seated)

Club Colours: Blue & white striped shirts, blue shorts

Nearest Railway Station: Sheffield (4 miles)

Parking (Car): Street Parking

Parking (Coach/Bus): Owlerton Stadium

Police Force and Tel No: South Yorkshire (0114 234 3131)

Disabled Visitors' Facilities
  Wheelchairs: North Stand
  Blind: Commentary available

Anticipated Development(s): Completion of work to South Stand, May 1996.

KEY

C Club Offices
S Club Shop
E Entrance(s) for visiting supporters

↑ North direction (approx)

❶ Leppings Lane
❷ River Dom
❸ A61 Penistone Road North
❹ Sheffield BR Station and City Centre (4 miles)
❺ Spion Kop
❻ To M1 (North)
❼ To M1 (South)

Left: Chris Waddle, now recovered from injury, is needed to be on form by Wednesday, to prevent a repeat of the 1994/95 season woes.

SHREWSBURY TOWN

Gay Meadow, Shrewsbury, SY2 6AB

Tel No: 01743 360111
Advance Tickets Tel No: 01743 360111
League: 2nd Division
Brief History: Founded 1886. Former Grounds: Monkmoor Racecourse, Ambler's Field & The Barracks Ground (moved to Gay Meadow in 1910). Elected to Football League in 1950. Record attendance 18,917
(Total) Current Capacity: 8,000 (3,000 seated)
Club Colours: Blue with White collar shirts, blue shorts.
snorts.

Nearest Railway Station: Shrewsbury

Parking (Car): Adjacent car park

Parking (Coach/Bus): Gay Meadow

Police Force and Tel No: West Mercia (01743 232888)

Disabled Visitors' Facilities
  Wheelchairs: Alongside Pitch (as directed)
  Blind: No special facility

KEY

C Club Offices
S Club Shop
E Entrance(s) for visiting supporters
R Refreshment bars for visiting supporters
T Toilets for visiting supporters

↑ North direction (approx)

❶ Entrance road to ground
❷ Abbey Foregate
❸ River Severn
❹ Car Parks
❺ Shrewsbury BR Station (1 mile — shortest route)
❻ Riverside enclosure

150

Right: The impressive Ian Stevens flexes his muscles during the Shrews 3-0 home victory over Bournemouth during October 1994.

SOUTHAMPTON

The Dell, Milton Road, Southampton, SO15 2XH

Tel No: 01703 220505
Advance Tickets Tel No: 01703 228575
League: F.A. Premier
Brief History: Founded 1885 as 'Southampton St. Mary's Young Mens Association' (changed name to Southampton in 1897). Former Grounds: Northlands Road, Antelope Ground, County Ground, moved to The Dell in 1898. Founder-members Third Division (1920). Record attendance 31,044.
(Total) Current Capacity: 15,000 (all seated)
Visiting Supporters' Allocation: 1,500 (all seated)

Club Colours: Red & white shirts, black shorts
Nearest Railway Station: Southampton
Parking (Car): Street parking
Parking (Coach/Bus): As directed by Police
Police Force and Tel No: Hampshire (01703 581111)
Disabled Visitors' Facilities
 Wheelchairs: Milton Road (book in advance)
 Blind: Commentary available (book in advance)

KEY
C Club Offices
S Club Shop
E Entrance(s) for visiting supporters
R Refreshment bars for visiting supporters
T Toilets for visiting supporters

⬆ North direction (approx)

❶ Archers Road
❷ Milton Road
❸ Hill Lane
❹ To Southampton BR station
❺ To A33, M3 and the north

Right: Known to Saints fans as 'God', Matthew Le Tissier entertains the Elland Road fans during a Premiership game in January, but he has still to convince Terry Venables he's worth a regular England place.

SOUTHEND UNITED

Roots Hall Ground, Victoria Avenue, Southend-on-Sea, SS2 6NQ

Tel No: 01702 340707
Advance Tickets Tel No: 01702 435602
League: 1st Division
Brief History: Founded 1906. Former Grounds: Roots Hall, Kursaal, The Stadium Grainger Road, moved to Roots Hall (new Ground) 1955. Founder-members Third Division (1920). Record attendance 31,033.
(Total) Current Capacity: 13,332 (all seated)

Club Colours: Blue with yellow trim shirts, yellow shorts
Nearest Railway Station: Prittlewell
Parking (Car): Street parking
Parking (Coach/Bus): Car park at Ground
Police Force and Tel No: Essex (01702 431212)
Disabled Visitors' Facilities
  Wheelchairs: West Stand
  Blind: Commentary available

KEY

C Club Offices
E Entrance(s) for visiting supporters

↑ North direction (approx)

❶ Director's Car Park
❷ Prittlewell BR Station (¼ mile)
❸ A127 Victoria Avenue
❹ Fairfax Drive
❺ Southend centre (½ mile)
❻ North Bank

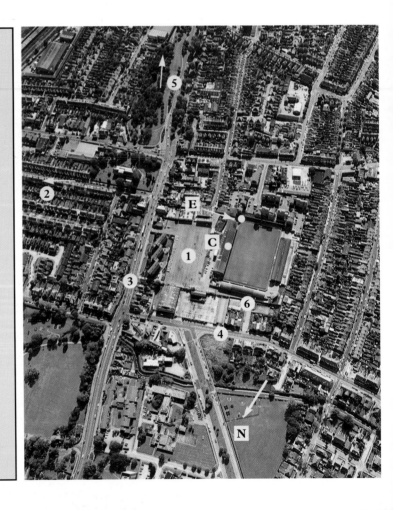

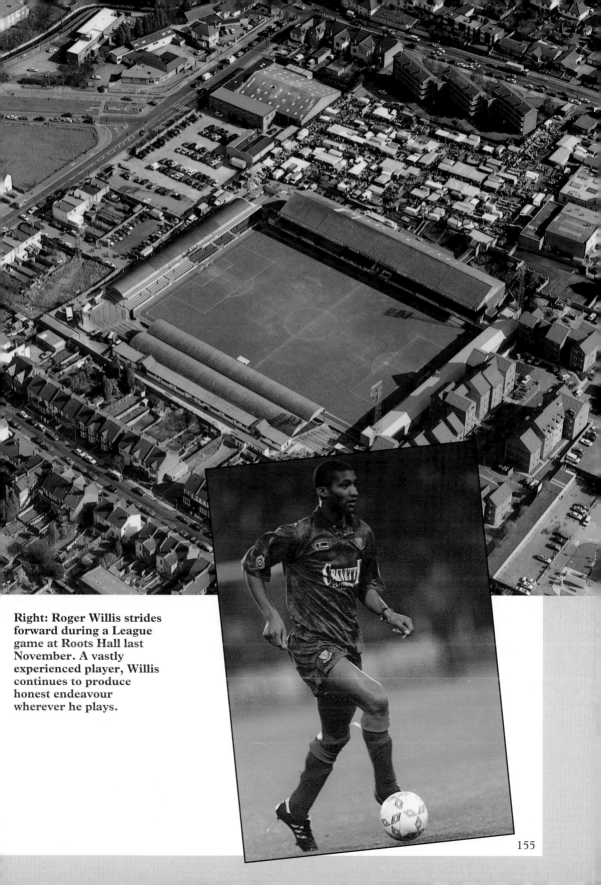

Right: Roger Willis strides forward during a League game at Roots Hall last November. A vastly experienced player, Willis continues to produce honest endeavour wherever he plays.

STOCKPORT COUNTY

Edgeley Park, Hardcastle Road, Edgeley, Stockport, SK3 9DD

Tel No: 0161 480 8888
Advance Tickets Tel No: 0161 480 8888
League: 2nd Division
Brief History: Founded 1883 as Heaton Norris Rovers, changed name to Stockport County in 1890. Former Grounds: Heaton Norris Recreation Ground, Heaton Norris Wanderers Cricket Ground, Chorlton's Farm, Ash Inn Ground, Wilkes Field (Belmont Street) and Nursery Inn (Green Lane), moved to Edgeley Park in 1902. Record attendance 27,833.
(Total) Current Capacity: 8,020 (4,200 seated)
Club Colours: Blue shirts with red & white flashes, white shorts

Nearest Railway Station: Stockport
Parking (Car): Street parking
Parking (Coach/Bus): As directed by Police
Police Force and Tel No: Greater Manchester (0161 872 5050)
Disabled Visitors' Facilities
　Wheelchairs: Main Stand
　Blind: Headsets available
Anticipated Development(s): (Editor's note: Substantial changes made, update information not advised.)

KEY
C Club Offices
E Entrance(s) for visiting supporters
R Refreshment bars for visiting supporters
T Toilets for visiting supporters

↑ North direction (approx)

❶ Mercian Way
❷ Hardcastle Road
❸ Stockport BR Station (¼ mile)
❹ Railway End
❺ Main Stand

Left: Kevin Francis
pictured early in the 1994/95
season, before his January
move to Birmingham City.
His departure no doubt
played a large part in
County's eventually
disappointing season.

STOKE CITY

Victoria Ground, Boothen Old Road, Stoke-on-Trent, ST4 4EG

Tel No: 01782 413511
Advance Tickets Tel No: 01782 413961
League: 1st Division
Brief History: Founded 1863 as Stoke F.C., amalgamated with Stoke Victoria in 1878, changed to Stoke City in 1925. Former Ground: Sweetings Field, moved to Victoria Ground in 1878. Founder-members Football League (1888). Record attendance 51,380.
(Total) Current Capacity: Approx. 23,500 (approx. 9,000 seated)

Club Colours: Red & white striped shirts, white shorts
Nearest Railway Station: Stoke-on-Trent
Parking (Car): Car park at ground
Parking (Coach/Bus): Whieldon Road
Police Force and Tel No: Staffordshire (01784 744644)
Disabled Visitors' Facilities
  Wheelchairs: Corner Butler Street/Boothen End
  Blind: Limited facilities (contact first)

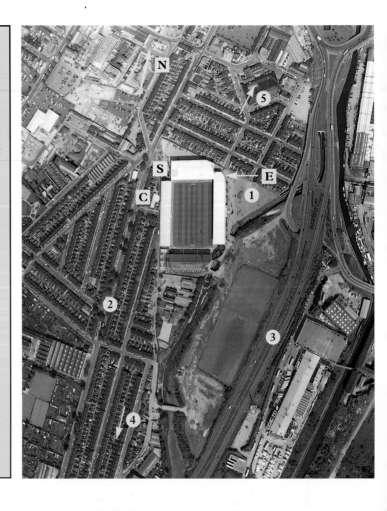

KEY
- **C** Club Offices
- **S** Club Shop
- **E** Entrance(s) for visiting supporters

↑ North direction (approx)

❶ Car Park
❷ Campbell Road
❸ A500 Queensway
❹ M6 Junction 15 (4 miles via A500)
❺ Stoke-on-Trent BR Station (¹/₂ mile)

Left: After trials with a couple of sides, Paul Allen seems to have settled in at the Potteries and much is expected of him and the side for 1995/96.

SUNDERLAND

Roker Park, Grantham Road, Roker, Sunderland, SR6 9SW

Tel No: 0191 514 0332

Advance Tickets Tel No: 0191 514 0332

League: 1st Division

Brief History: Founded 1879 as 'Sunderland and District Teachers Association', changed to 'Sunderland Association' (in 1880) and shortly after to 'Sunderland'. Former Grounds: Blue House Field, Groves Field (Ashbrooke), Horatio Street, Abbs Field & Newcastle Road, moved to Roker Park in 1898. Record attendance 75,118

(Total) Current Capacity: 22,657 (7,811 seated)

Club Colours: Red & white striped shirts, black shorts

Nearest Railway Station: Seaburn

Parking (Car): Car park adjacent ground

Parking (Coach/Bus): Seafront, Roker

Police Force and Tel No: Northumbria (0191 567 6155)

Disabled Visitors' Facilities
  Wheelchairs: Roker Baths Road
  Blind: Commentary available

Anticipated Development(s): Possible move to new 48,000 all-seater Stadium, 1996/97 season.

KEY

C Club Offices

S Club Shop

E Entrance(s) for visiting supporters

↑ North direction (approx)

❶ Roker Baths Road
❷ Grantham Road
❸ Seaburn BR Station (1 mile)
❹ To A1018 Newcastle Road
❺ Hampden Road
❻ To A183 Roker Terrace (Seafront)
❼ Car Park

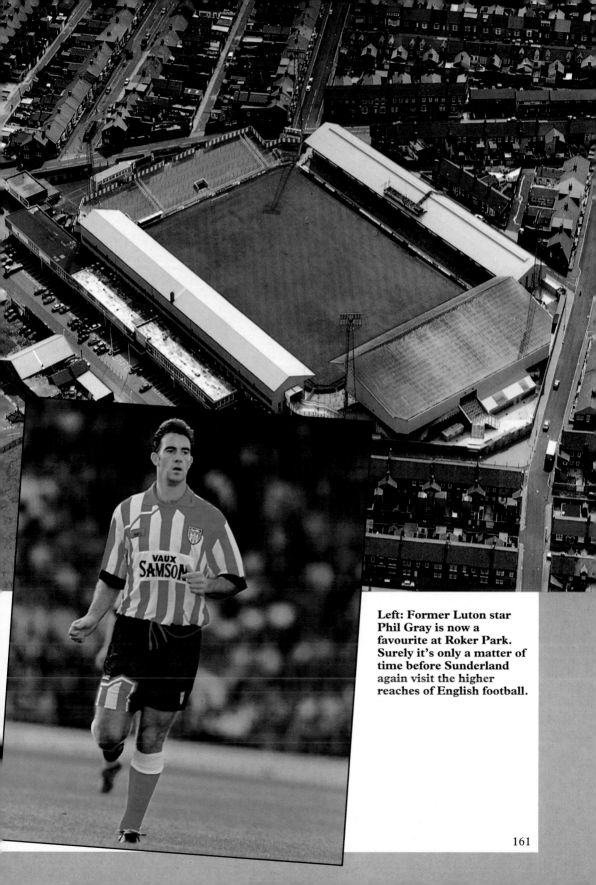

Left: Former Luton star Phil Gray is now a favourite at Roker Park. Surely it's only a matter of time before Sunderland again visit the higher reaches of English football.

SWANSEA CITY

Vetch Field, Swansea, SA1 3SU

Tel No: 01792 474114
Advance Tickets Tel No: 01792 474114
League: 2nd Division
Brief History: Founded 1900 as Swansea Town, changed to Swansea City in 1970. Former Grounds: various, including Recreation Ground. Moved to Vetch Field in 1912. Founder-members Third Division (1920). Record attendance 32,796.
(Total) Current Capacity: 16,419 (3,414 seated)
Club Colours: White shirts, white shorts

Nearest Railway Station: Swansea High Street
Parking (Car): Kingsway car park & adjacent Clarence Terrace, (supervised car park).
Parking (Coach/Bus): As directed by Police
Police Force and Tel No: South Wales (01792 456999)
Disabled Visitors' Facilities
　Wheelchairs: Glamorgan Street
　Blind: No special facility
Anticipated Development(s): Possible move to new Stadium in 1996/97.

KEY
C Club Offices
S Club Shop
E Entrance(s) for visiting supporters

↑ North direction (approx)

❶ Glamorgan Street
❷ William Street
❸ Richardson Street
❹ A4067 Oystermouth Road (8 miles to M4 Junction 42)
❺ Swansea High Street BR Station (½ mile)
❻ Supervised Car Park
❼ North Bank

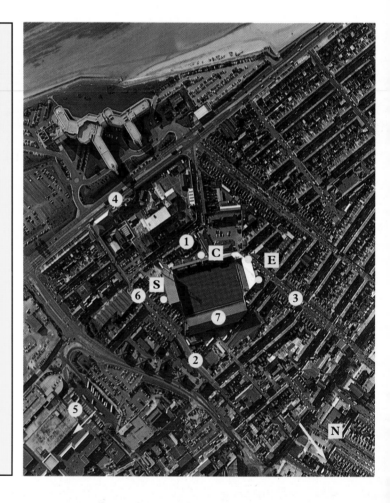

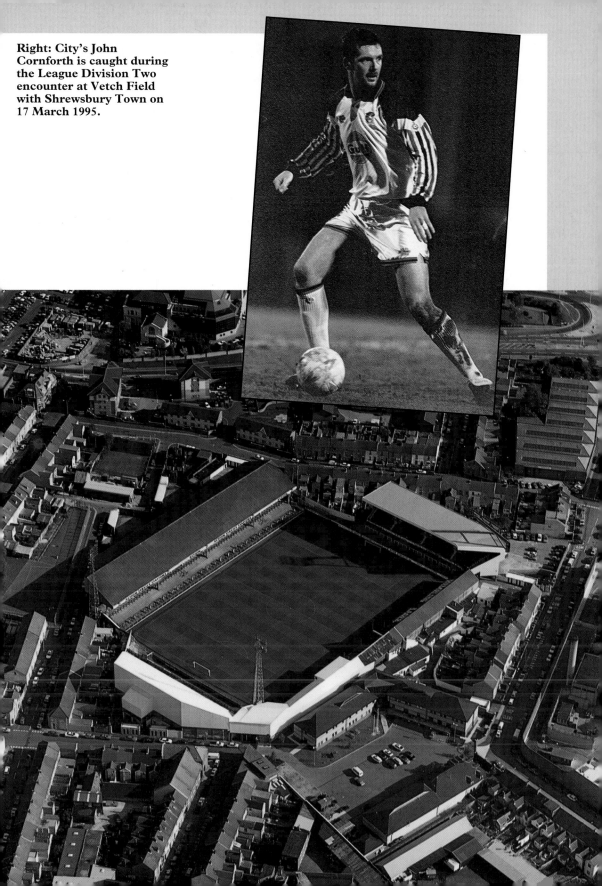

Right: City's John Cornforth is caught during the League Division Two encounter at Vetch Field with Shrewsbury Town on 17 March 1995.

SWINDON TOWN

County Ground, County Road, Swindon, SN1 2ED

Tel No: 01793 430430

Advance Tickets Tel No: 01793 430430

League: 2nd Division

Brief History: Founded 1881. Former Grounds: Quarry Ground, Globe Field, Croft Ground, County Ground (adjacent current to Ground and now Cricket Ground), moved to current County Ground in 1896. Founder-members Third Division (1920). Record attendance 32,000

(Total) Current Capacity: 19,000 (all seated)

Visiting Supporters' Allocation: 3,000 (all seated)

Club Colours: Red shirts, red shorts

Nearest Railway Station: Swindon

Parking (Car): Town Centre

Parking (Coach/Bus): Adjacent car park

Police Force and Tel No: Wiltshire (01793 528111)

Disabled Visitors' Facilities
 Wheelchairs: Intel Stand
 Blind: Commentary available

KEY

C Club Offices

S Club Shop

E Entrance(s) for visiting supporters

R Refreshment bars for visiting supporters

T Toilets for visiting supporters

↑ North direction (approx)

❶ Shrivenham Road
❷ County Road
❸ A345 Queens Drive (M4 Junction 15 – 3¹/2 miles)
❹ Swindon BR Station (¹/2 mile)
❺ Town End
❻ Car Park
❼ County Cricket Ground

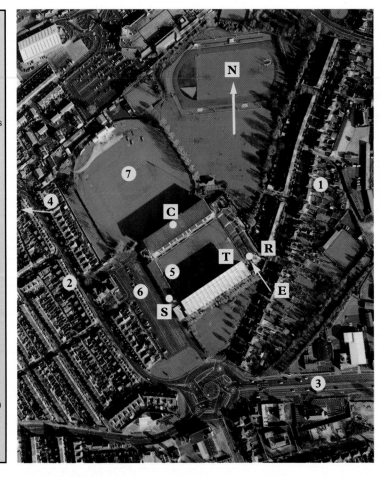

Right: Even International defender Luc Nijholt could not prevent back to back relegations for Swindon. Perhaps this is one way of preventing opposing forwards getting the ball!

TORQUAY UNITED

Plainmoor Ground, Torquay, TQ1 3PS

Tel No: 01803 328666
Advance Tickets Tel No: 01803 328666
League: 3rd Division
Brief History: Founded 1898, as Torquay United, amalgamated with Ellacombe in 1910, changed name to Torquay Town. Amalgamated with Babbacombe in 1921, changed name to Torquay United. Former grounds: Teignmouth Road, Torquay Recreation Ground, Cricketfield Road & Torquay Cricket Ground, moved to Plainmoor (Ellacombe Ground) in 1910. Record attendance 21,908.
(Total) Current Capacity: 6,455 (2,324 seated)
Visiting Supporters' Allocation: 1,248 (200 seated)

Club Colours: Yellow with navy & white stripe shirts, navy shorts

Nearest Railway Station: Torquay (2 miles)

Parking (Car): Street parking

Parking (Coach/Bus): Lymington Road coach station

Police Force and Tel No: Devon & Cornwall (01803 214491)

Disabled Visitors' Facilities
Wheelchairs: Main Office
Blind: Commentary available

KEY
C	Club Offices
S	Club Shop
E	Entrance(s) for visiting supporters
R	Refreshment bars for visiting supporters
T	Toilets for visiting supporters

↑ North direction (approx)

❶ Warbro Road
❷ B3202 Marychurch Road
❸ Marnham Road
❹ Torquay BR Station (2 miles)

Left: A low key pre-season friendly match in August, sees United's Tom Kelly apparently concentrating in anticipation for the season ahead.

TOTTENHAM HOTSPUR

White Hart Lane, 748 High Road, Tottenham, London N17 0AP

Tel No: 0181 808 6666

Advance Tickets Tel No: 0181 808 8080

League: F. A. Premier

Brief History: Founded 1882 as 'Hotspur', changed name to Tottenham Hotspur in 1885. Former Grounds: Tottenham Marshes and Northumberland Park, moved to White Hart Lane in 1899. F. A. Cup winner 1901 (as a non-League club). Record attendance 75,038

(Total) Current Capacity: 33,740 (25,883 seated)

Visiting Supporters' Allocation: 2,481

Club Colours: White shirts, navy blue shorts

Nearest Railway Station: White Hart Lane plus Seven Sisters & Manor House (tube)

Parking (Car): Street parking (min ¼ mile from ground)

Parking (Coach/Bus): Northumberland Park coach park

Police Force and Tel No: Metropolitan (0181 801 3443)

Disabled Visitors' Facilities
  Wheelchairs: Paxton Road and High Road (by prior arrangement)
  Blind: No special facility

KEY

- **C** Club Offices
- **S** Club Shop
- **E** Entrance(s) for visiting supporters
- **R** Refreshment bars for visiting supporters
- **T** Toilets for visiting supporters

↑ North direction (approx)

- ❶ Park Lane
- ❷ A1010 High Road
- ❸ White Hart Lane BR Station
- ❹ Paxton Road
- ❺ Worcester Avenue
- ❻ West Stand

Left: Bristolian Gary Mabbutt, in early season action for 'Spurs, was to later suffer, and recover from, an horrific and controversial match injury.

TRANMERE ROVERS

Prenton Park, Prenton Road West, Birkenhead, L42 9PN

Tel No: 0151 608 3677

Advance Tickets Tel No: 0151 608 3677

League: 1st Division

Brief History: Founded 1884 as Belmont F.C., changed name to Tranmere Rovers in 1885 (not connected to earlier 'Tranmere Rovers'). Former grounds: Steele's Field and Ravenshaw's Field (also known as Old Prenton Park, ground of Tranmere Rugby Club), moved to (new) Prenton Park in 1911. Founder-members 3rd Division North (1921). Record attendance 24,424.

(Total) Current capacity: 16,788 (all seated)

Visiting Supporters' Allocation: Between 2,000 and 5,823 (all seated)

Club Colours: White shirts, white shorts

Nearest Railway Station: Hamilton Square or Rock Ferry

Parking (Car): Car park at Ground

Parking (Coach/Bus): Car park at Ground

Police Force and Tel No: Merseyside (0151 709 6010)

Disabled Visitors' Facilities
  Wheelchairs: Main Stand
  Blind: No special facility

KEY

C Club Offices
S Club Shop
E Entrance(s) for visiting supporters
R Refreshment bars for visiting supporters
T Toilets for visiting supporters

↑ North direction (approx)

❶ Car Park
❷ Prenton Road West
❸ Borough Road
❹ M53 Junction 4 (B5151) – 3 miles
❺ Birkenhead (1 mile)

Right: Arguably the buy of the decade of any Endsleigh League club, John 'Aldo' Aldridge continues to purge defences in Division One and at International level for the Republic of Ireland.

WALSALL

Bescot Stadium, Bescot Crescent, Walsall, West Midlands, WS1 4SA

Tel No: 01922 22791
Advance Tickets Tel No: 01922 22791
League: 3rd Division
Brief History: Founded 1888 as Walsall Town Swifts (amalgamation of Walsall Town - founded 1884 - and Walsall Swifts - founded 1885), changed name to Walsall in 1895. Former Grounds: The Chuckery, West Bromwich Road (twice), Hilary Street (later named Fellows Park, twice), moved to Bescot Stadium in 1990. Founder-members Second Division (1892). Record attendance 10,628 (24,100 at Fellows Park).

(Total) Current Capacity: 9,485 (6,685 seated)
Visiting Supporters' Allocation: 1,916 (1,916 seated)
Club Colours: Red shirts, White shorts
Nearest Railway Station: Bescot
Parking (Car): Car park at Ground
Parking (Coach/Bus): Car park at Ground
Police Force and Tel No : West Midlands (01922 38111)
Disabled Visitors' Facilities
  Wheelchairs: Highgate Stand
  Blind: Commentary planned

KEY

C Club Offices
S Club Shop
E Entrance(s) for visiting supporters
R Refreshment bars for visiting supporters
T Toilets for visiting supporters

↑ North direction (approx)

❶ Motorway M6
❷ M6 Junction 9
❸ Bescot BR Station
❹ Car Parks
❺ Bescot Crescent

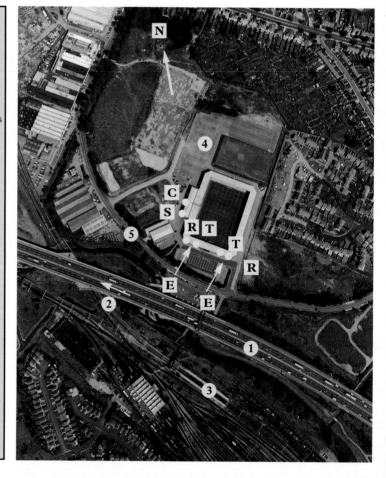

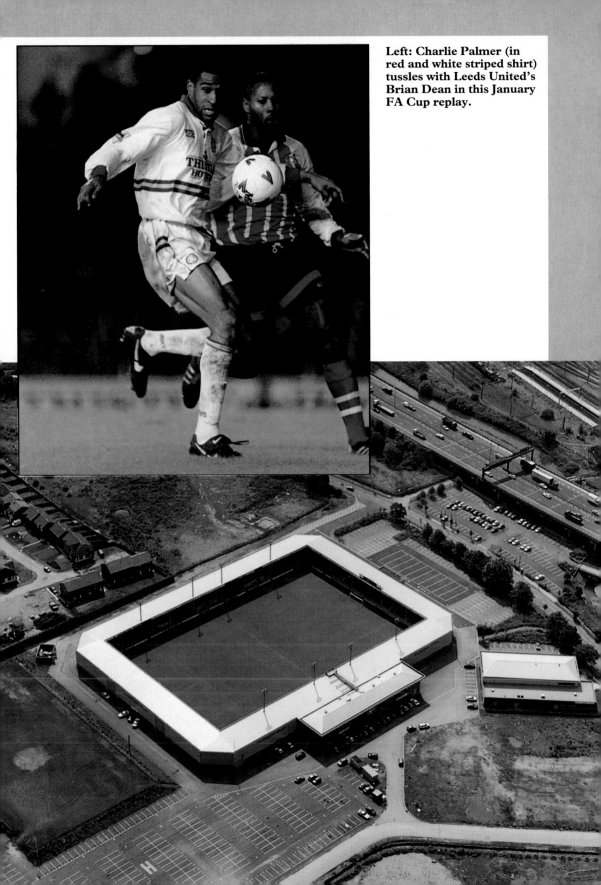

Left: Charlie Palmer (in red and white striped shirt) tussles with Leeds United's Brian Dean in this January FA Cup replay.

WATFORD

Vicarage Road Stadium, Watford, WD1 8ER

Tel No: 01923 230933
Advance Tickets Tel No: 01923 220393
League: 1st Division
Brief History: Founded 1898 as an amalgamation of West Herts (founded 1891) and Watford St. Mary's (founded early 1890s). Former Grounds: Wiggenhall Road (Watford St. Mary's) and West Herts Sports Ground, moved to Vicarage Road in 1922. Founder-members Third Division (1920). Record attendance 34,099.
(Total) Current Capacity: 22,000 (Anticipated 1995/96 season)
Club Colours: Yellow shirts with black collar & shoulder panel, Black shorts with yellow & red trim.

Nearest Railway Station: Watford High Street or Watford Junction.

Parking (Car): Nearby multi-storey car park in town centre (10 mins walk)

Parking (Coach/Bus): Cardiff Road car park

Police Force and Tel No: Hertfordshire (01923 244444)

Disabled Visitors' Facilities

Wheelchairs: Corner East Stand and South Stand (special enclosure for approx. 24 wheelchairs), plus enclosure in North East Corner

Blind: Commentary available in the East Stand (20 seats, free of charge)

KEY	
C Club Offices	
S Club Shop	
E Entrance(s) for visiting supporters	
R Refreshment bars for visiting supporters	
T Toilets for visiting supporters	

↑ North direction (approx)

❶ Vicarage Road
❷ Occupation Road
❸ Rous Stand
❹ Town Centre (½ mile) – Car Parks, High Street BR Station

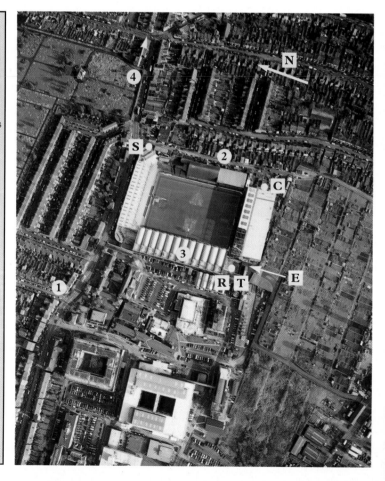

Right: Lee Nogan pictured in the Hornets' colours before his move to Reading. Not a regular for Watford during the season, Nogan proved what a quality player he is in Reading's Play-Off near-miss at Wembley.

WEST BROMWICH ALBION

The Hawthorns, Halfords Lane, West Bromwich, West Midlands, B71 4LF

Tel No: 0121 525 8888
Advance Tickets Tel No: 0121 553 5472
League: 1st Division
Brief History: Founded 1879. Former Grounds: Coopers Hill, Dartmouth Park, Four Acres, Stoney Lane, moved to the Hawthorns in 1900. Founder-members of Football League (1888). Record attendance 64,815.
(Total) Current Capacity: 26,000 (all seated)
Club Colours: Navy blue & white striped shirts, white shorts

Nearest Railway Station: Rolfe Street, Smethwick (1½ miles)
Parking (Car): Halfords Lane & Rainbow Stand car parks.
Parking (Coach/Bus): Rainbow Stand car park
Police Force and Tel No: West Midlands (0121 554 3414)
Disabled Visitors' Facilities
  Wheelchairs: Corner Birmingham Road/Main Stand
  Blind: Facility available

KEY

C Club Offices
S Club Shop
E Entrance(s) for visiting supporters
T Toilets for visiting supporters

↑ North direction (approx)

❶ A41 Birmingham Road
❷ M5 Junction 1
❸ Birmingham centre (4 miles)
❹ Halfords Lane
❺ Main Stand
❻ Smethwick End
❼ Rolfe Street, Smethwick BR Station (1½ miles)
❽ The Hawthorns BR Station

Left: Former Manchester United midfielder Mike Phelan now plays his football at The Hawthorns. He is seen here celebrating his scoring of a goal – a not too regular occurrence!

WEST HAM UNITED

Boleyn Ground, Green Street, Upton Park, London, E13 9AZ

Tel No: 0181 472 2740
Advance Tickets Tel No: 0181 472 3322
League: F. A. Premier
Brief History: Founded 1895 as Thames Ironworks, changed name to West Ham United in 1900. Former Grounds: Hermit Road, Browning Road, The Memorial Ground, moved to Boleyn Ground in 1904. Record attendance 42,322.
(Total) Current Capacity: 22,503 (11,600 seated)
Visiting Supporters' Allocation: 3,000 (500 seated)
Club Colours: Claret & blue shirts, white shorts.

Nearest Railway Station: Barking BR, Upton Park (tube)
Parking (Car): Street parking
Parking (Coach/Bus): As directed by police
Police Force and Tel No: Metropolitan (0181 593 8232)
Disabled Visitors' Facilities
   Wheelchairs: Green Street
   Blind: No special facility
Development(s): (Editor's note: Updated information regarding ground not advised.)

KEY

C Club Offices
S Club Shop
E Entrance(s) for visiting supporters
R Refreshment bars for visiting supporters
T Toilets for visiting supporters

↑ North direction (approx)

❶ A124 Barking Road
❷ Green Street
❸ North Bank
❹ Upton Park Tube Station (¼ mile)
❺ Barking BR Station (1 mile)

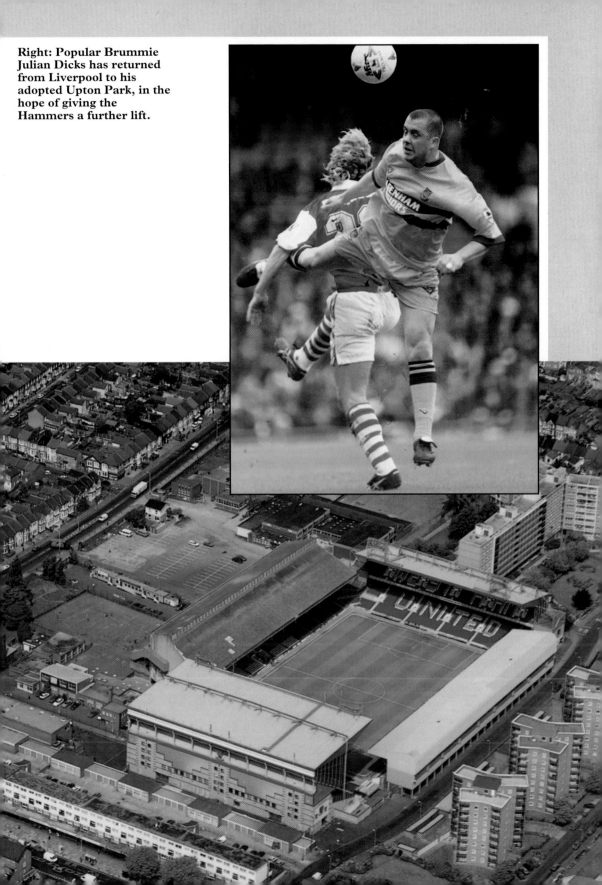

Right: Popular Brummie
Julian Dicks has returned
from Liverpool to his
adopted Upton Park, in the
hope of giving the
Hammers a further lift.

WIGAN ATHLETIC

Springfield Park, Wigan, Lancs, WN6 7BA

Tel No: 01942 244433
Advance Tickets Tel No: 01942 244433
League: 3rd Division
Brief History: Founded 1932. Springfield Park used by former club Wigan Borough (Football League 1921-31) but unrelated to current club. Elected to Football League in 1978 (the last club to be elected rather than promoted). Record attendance 27,500.
(Total) Current Capacity: 6,674 (1,109 seated)
Visiting Supporters' Allocation: 1,600 (300 seated)

Club Colours: Blue and white stripes shirt, blue shorts
Nearest Railway Station: Wallgate and North Western (1 mile)
Parking (Car): Street parking
Parking (Coach/Bus): At Ground
Police Force and Tel No: Greater Manchester (01942 244981)
Disabled Visitors' Facilities
  Wheelchairs: Phoenix Stand side
  Blind: Commentary available, book in advance and bring own headphones.

KEY

C Club Offices
S Club Shop
E Entrance(s) for visiting supporters
R Refreshment bars for visiting supporters
T Toilets for visiting supporters

↑ North direction (approx)

❶ Private Car Park
❷ Springfield Road
❸ St. Andrews Drive
❹ Wallgate and North Western BR Stations (1 mile)
❺ B5375 Woodhouse Lane

Left: Captured here in similar colours to Inter Milan, Wigan's Neil Morton exhibits the ball skills more usually seen at the San Siro!

WIMBLEDON

Selhurst Park, London, SE25 6PU

Tel No: 0181 771 2233

Advance Tickets Tel No: 0181 771 8841

League: F.A. Premier

Brief History: Founded 1889 as Wimbledon Old Centrals, changed name to Wimbledon in 1905. Former Grounds: Wimbledon Common, Pepy's Road, Grand Drive, Merton Hall Road, Malden Wanderers Cricket Ground & Plough Lane. Moved to Selhurst Park (Crystal Palace F.C. Ground) in 1991. Elected to Football League in 1977. Record attendance (Plough Lane) 18,000.

(Total) Current Capacity: 26,000 (all seated)

Visiting Supporters' Allocation: Approx 2,500

Club Colours: Blue shirts, blue shorts

Nearest Railway Station: Selhurst, Norwood Junction & Thornton Heath

Parking (Car): Street parking & Sainsbury's car park

Parking (Coach/Bus): Thornton Heath

Police Force and Tel No: Metropolitan (0181 649 1391)

Disabled Visitors' Facilities

Wheelchairs: Park Road

Blind: Commentary available

Anticipated Development(s): New stand, Holmesdale Road, End, opening August 1995.

KEY	
C	Club Offices
S	Club Shop
E	Entrance(s) for visiting supporters
T	Toilets for visiting supporters

⬆ North direction (approx)

❶ Whitehorse Lane
❷ Park Road
❸ A213 Selhurst Road
❹ Selhurst BR Station (¹/₂ mile)
❺ Norwood Junction BR Station (¹/₄ mile)
❻ Thornton Heath BR Station (¹/₂ mile)
❼ Car Park (Sainsbury's)

Right: Another from the Dons' conveyor belt of quality players – Warren Barton is seen here in Dons attire, before his £4 million move to Tyneside in May 1995.

WOLVERHAMPTON WANDERERS

Molineux Ground, Waterloo Road, Wolverhampton, WV1 4QR

Tel No: 01902 655000

Advance Tickets Tel No: 01902 653653

League: 1st Division

Brief History: Founded 1877 as St. Lukes, combined with Goldthorn Hill to become Wolverhampton Wanderers in 1884. Former Grounds: Old Windmill Field, John Harper's Field and Dudley Road, moved to Molineux in 1889. Founder-members Football League (1888). Record attendance 61,315

(Total) Current Capacity: 28,500 (all seated)

Visiting Supporters' Allocation: 1,500 minimum

Club Colours: Gold shirts, black shorts

Nearest Railway Station: Wolverhampton

Parking (Car): West Park and adjacent North Bank

Parking (Coach/Bus): As directed by Police

Police Force and Tel No: West Midlands (01902 27851)

Disabled Visitors' Facilities
  Wheelchairs: North Bank
  Blind: Commentary (by prior arrangement).

Anticipated Development(s): (Editor's note: Updated information regarding ground not advised.)

KEY

C Club Offices

S Club Shop

E Entrance(s) for visiting supporters

R Refreshment bars for visiting supporters

T Toilets for visiting supporters

↑ North direction (approx)

❶ Stan Cullis Stand
❷ John Ireland Stand
❸ Billy Wright Stand
❹ Ring Road – St. Peters
❺ Waterloo Road
❻ A449 Stafford Street
❼ BR Station (1/2 mile)

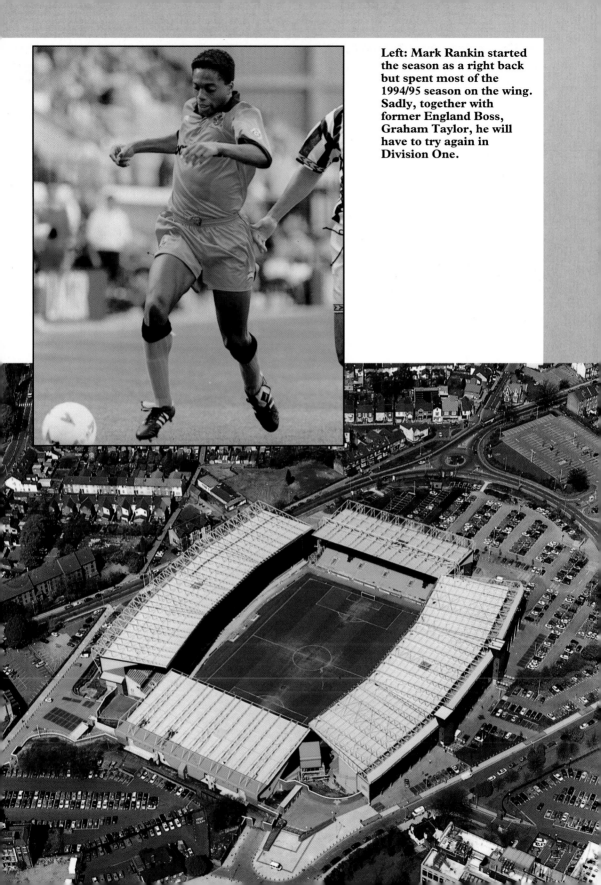

Left: Mark Rankin started the season as a right back but spent most of the 1994/95 season on the wing. Sadly, together with former England Boss, Graham Taylor, he will have to try again in Division One.

WREXHAM

Racecourse Ground, Mold Road, Wrexham, Clwyd LL11 2AN

Tel No: 01978 262129
Advance Tickets Tel No: 01978 262129
League: 2nd Division
Brief History: Founded 1873 (oldest Football Club in Wales). Former Ground: Acton Park, permanent move to Racecourse Ground c.1900. Founder-members Third Division North (1921). Record attendance 34,445.
(Total) Current Capacity: 12,500 (5,026 seated)
Visiting Supporters' Allocation: 2,680 (2,230 seated)

Club Colours: Red shirts, white shorts

Nearest Railway Station: Wrexham General

Parking (Car): (Nearby) Town car parks

Parking (Coach/Bus): As directed by Police

Police Force and Tel No: Wrexham Division (01978 290222)

Disabled Visitors' Facilities
  Wheelchairs: Mold Road Side
  Blind: Commentary available

KEY

C Club Offices
S Club Shop
E Entrance(s) for visiting supporters
R Refreshment bars for visiting supporters
T Toilets for visiting supporters

↑ North direction (approx)

❶ Wrexham General BR Station
❷ A541 – Mold Road
❸ Wrexham Town Centre
❹ Car Park
❺ Kop Town End

Right: Gary Bennett seen in familiar pose for Wrexham. This exciting forward finished top of the country's goal charts but lacked goalscoring support from his Welsh colleagues.

WYCOMBE WANDERERS

Adams Park, Hillbottom Road, Sands, High Wycombe, Bucks, HP12 4HU.

Tel No: 01494 472100
Advance Tickets Tel No: 01494 472100
League: 3rd Division
Brief History: Founded 1884. Former Grounds: The Rye, Spring Meadows, Loakes Park, moved to Adams Park 1990. Promoted to Football League 1993. Record attendance 15,678 (Loakes Park)
(Total) Current Capacity: 9,600 (1,267 seated)
Visiting Supporters' Allocation: 2,200 (standing)
Club Colours: Cambridge and Oxford blue quartered shirts, blue shorts.

Nearest Railway Station: High Wycombe (2$^{1}/_{2}$ miles)
Parking (Car): At Ground and Street parking
Parking (Coach/Bus): At Ground
Police Force and Tel No: Thames Valley 01296 396534
Disabled Visitors' Facilities
  Wheelchairs: Special shelter - Main Stand, Hillbottom Road end
  Blind: Commentary available
Anticipated Development(s): New all-seater stand with executive boxes on South side.

KEY
C	Club Offices
S	Club Shop
E	Entrance(s) for visiting supporters
R	Refreshment bars for visiting supporters
T	Toilets for visiting supporters

↑ North direction (approx)

❶ Car Park
❷ Hillbottom Road (Industrial Estate)
❸ M40 Junction 4 (approx. 2 miles)
❹ Wycombe Town Centre (approx. 2$^{1}/_{2}$ miles)

Left: Wycombe's Jason Cousins seems to have suppressed his impetuous nature and is now attracting the attentions of both Premier and Welsh National team scouts.

YORK CITY

Bootham Crescent, York, YO3 7AQ

Tel No: 01904 624447
Advance Tickets Tel No: 01904 624447
League: 2nd Division
Brief History: Founded 1922. Former ground: Fulfordgate Ground, moved to Bootham Crescent in 1932. Record attendance 28,123.
(Total) Current Capacity: 12,475 (3,245 seated)
Visiting Supporters' Allocation: 3,980 (630 seated)

Club Colours: Red shirts, blue shorts
Nearest Railway Station: York
Parking (Car): Street parking
Parking (Coach/Bus): As directed by Police
Police Force and Tel No: North Yorkshire (01904 631321)
Disabled Visitors' Facilities
  Wheelchairs: In front of Family Stand
  Blind: Commentary available

KEY

C Club Offices
S Club Shop
E Entrance(s) for visiting supporters
R Refreshment bars for visiting supporters
T Toilets for visiting supporters

↑ North direction (approx)

❶ Bootham Crescent
❷ Grosvenor Road
❸ Burton Stone Lane
❹ York BR Station (1 mile)

Right: Former City trainee Scott Jordan was unable to command a regular place in the side, and the team as a whole didn't quite produce the goods.

HAMPDEN STADIUM

Hampden Park, Letherby Drive, Mount Florida, Glasgow, G42 9BA

Tel No: 0141 632 1275
Brief History: Opened on 31 October, 1903 and used since as the Home Ground of Queen's Park F.C. (the oldest club in Scotland). Used extensively for Scottish International matches. Record attendance: 150,239 (Scotland v England, April 1937).
(Total) Current Capacity: 35,000 (all seated)
Nearest Railway Station: Mount Florida or Kings Park

Parking (Car): Adjacent car park
Parking (Coach/Bus): Stadium car park.
Police Force and Tel No: Strathclyde 0141 422 1113
Disabled Visitors' Facilities
  Wheelchairs: Special Terrace
  Blind: Commentary available
Anticipated Development(s): Increase to 60,000 all seated in 1996.

KEY

❶ Somerville Drive
❷ Cathcart Road
❸ Aikenhead Road
❹ Mount Florida BR Station
❺ Kings Park BR Station (1/2 mile)
❻ Parking
❼ Main Entrance

Left: Gary McAlister has proved to be an inspirational captain for both Leeds United and Scotland. Although the Scots missed out on the 1994 World Cup, their current form makes them look likely candidates to qualify for the 1996 European Championships.

ABERDEEN

Pittodrie Stadium, Pittodrie Street, Aberdeen, AB2 1QH

Tel No: 01224 632328
League: Premier Division
Brief History: Founded 1881, amalgamated
with Orion and Victoria United in 1903,
Pittodrie Park used by the former Aberdeen
F.C. Record attendance: 45,061. Former
grounds: Links, Hayton, Holburn Cricket
Ground, Chanonry. Orion - Cattofield. Victoria
United - Central Park.
(Total) Current Capacity: 21,634 (all seated)
Club Colours: Red Shirts, Red Shorts.
Nearest Railway Station: Aberdeen

Parking (Car): Beach Boulevard, King Street &
Golf Road
Parking (Coach/Bus): Beach Boulevard
Police Force and Tel No: Grampian 01224
639111
Disabled Visitors' Facilities
  Wheelchairs: Merkland Stand (prior
  arrangement), Richard Donald Stand (season pass)
  Blind: No special facility.
Anticipated Development(s): (Editor's note:
  Update information regarding Ground not
  advised.)

KEY
C Club Offices
S Club Shop
E Entrance(s) for visiting
supporters
R Refreshment bars for visiting
supporters
T Toilets for visiting supporters

❶ Pittodrie Street
❷ Gold Road
❸ A92 King Street
❹ Aberdeen BR station (1 mile)
❺ Trinity Cemetery

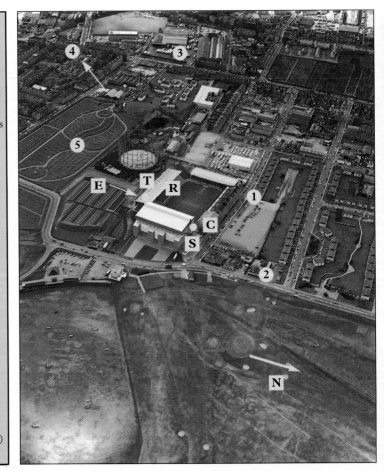

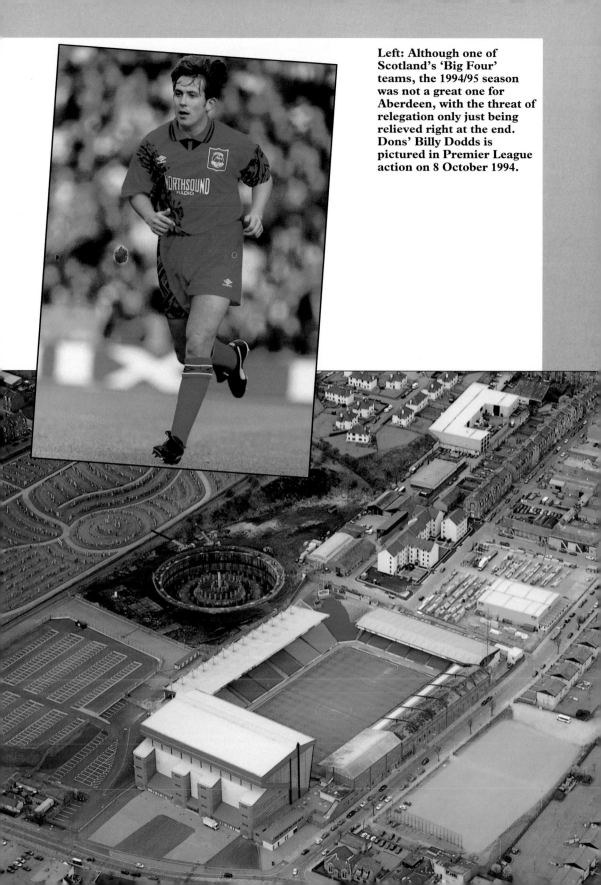

Left: Although one of Scotland's 'Big Four' teams, the 1994/95 season was not a great one for Aberdeen, with the threat of relegation only just being relieved right at the end. Dons' Billy Dodds is pictured in Premier League action on 8 October 1994.

CELTIC

Celtic Park, 95 Kerrydale Street, Glasgow, G40 3RE

Tel No: 0141 556 2611
Advance Tickets Tel No: 0141 551 8653
League: Premier Division
Brief History: Founded 1888. Former ground: (Old) Celtic Park until 1892. Founder members Scottish League (1890). Record attendance: 92,000.
(Total) Current Capacity: 34,000 (all seated)
Club Colours: Green & White Hooped Shirts, White Shorts
Nearest Railway Station: Bridgeton Cross

Parking (Car): Adjacent to ground.
Parking (Coach/Bus): Adjacent to ground.
Police Force and Tel No: Strathclyde 0141 554 1113
Disabled Visitors' Facilities
  Wheelchairs: North Enclosure (Permit Holders)
  Blind: Commentary available.
Anticipated Development(s): Ongoing phases of construction will produce a 60,000 capacity stadium when complete.

KEY
C Club Offices
S Club Shop

❶ A74 London Road
❷ A89 Gallowgate
❸ To Bridgeton Cross BR Station
❹ Springfield Road

Left: A more successful season for Celtic culminated in triumph at the Scottish Cup Final in May. Pictured on the day is Paul McStay. The new season promises much with a return to the much-rebuilt Celtic Park and the prospect of renewed European competition.

DUNDEE UNITED

Tannadice Park, Tannadice Street, Dundee, DD3 7JW

Tel No: 01382 833166
League: 1st Division
Brief History: Founded 1909 as Dundee
Hibernian, changed name to Dundee United in
1923. Tannadice Park used previously by
former Scottish League members (1894/95)
Dundee Wanderers. Record attendance 28,000.
(Total) Current Capacity: 16,868 (7,680
seated)
Club Colours: Tangerine Shirts, Black Shorts
Nearest Railway Station: Dundee

Parking (Car): Street Parking & Gussie Park
Parking (Coach/Bus): Gussie Park
Police Force and Tel No: Tayside 01382 23200
Disabled Visitors' Facilities
  Wheelchairs: George Fox Stand & Tannadice
Street
  Blind: Facility available
Anticipated Development(s): (Editor's note:
Update information regarding Ground not
advised.)

KEY

E Entrance(s) for visiting
supporters

❶ Dens Road
❷ Dundee F.C. Ground
❸ Sandemen Street
❹ Arklay Street
❺ Tannadice Street
❻ Dundee BR Station (1 mile)

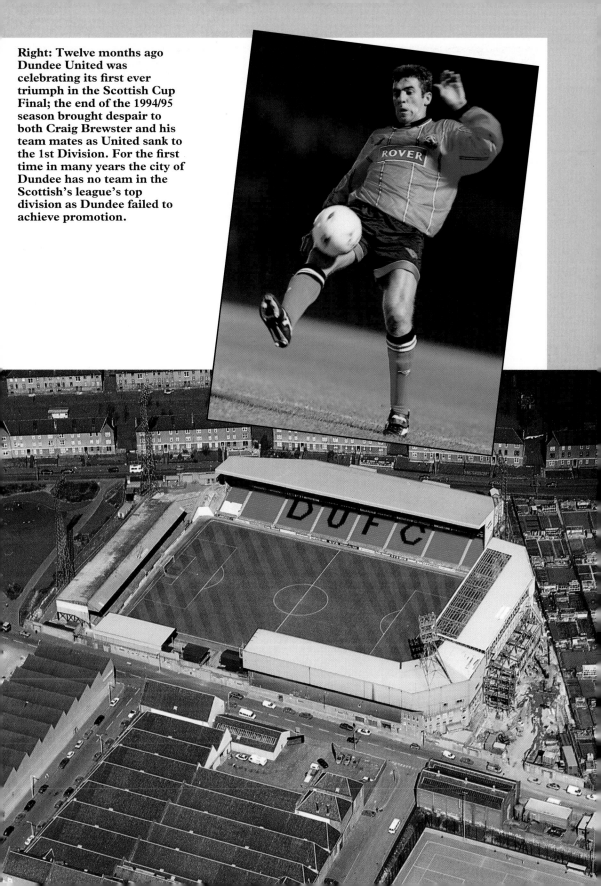

Right: Twelve months ago Dundee United was celebrating its first ever triumph in the Scottish Cup Final; the end of the 1994/95 season brought despair to both Craig Brewster and his team mates as United sank to the 1st Division. For the first time in many years the city of Dundee has no team in the Scottish's league's top division as Dundee failed to achieve promotion.

HEART OF MIDLOTHIAN

Tynecastle Park, Gorgie Road, Edinburgh, EH11 2NL

Tel No: 0131 337 6132
Advance Tickets Tel No: 0131 337 9011
League: Premier Division
Brief History: Founded 1874, founder members
Scottish League (1890). Former grounds: East
Meadows, moved to Powderhall in 1878,
Gorgie Road (1881), Tynecastle (1886).
Record attendance: 53,496.
(Total) Current Capacity: 13,500
Club Colours: Maroon Shirts, White Shorts.
Nearest Railway Station: Edinburgh
Haymarket

Parking (Car): Street Parking
Parking (Coach/Bus): Chesser Avenue
Police Force and Tel No: Lothian & Borders
0131 229 2323
Disabled Visitors' Facilities
Wheelchairs: 20 spaces total
Blind: Commentary available
Anticipated Development(s): Ongoing
reconstruction providing 19,000 capacity on
completion.

KEY

C Club Offices
S Club Shop
E Entrance(s) for visiting
supporters
R Refreshment bars for visiting
supporters
T Toilets for visiting supporters

❶ Gorgie Road
❷ McLeod Street
❸ West Approach Road
❹ To Edinburgh Haymarket
BR station
❺ Murrayfield Rugby Stadium

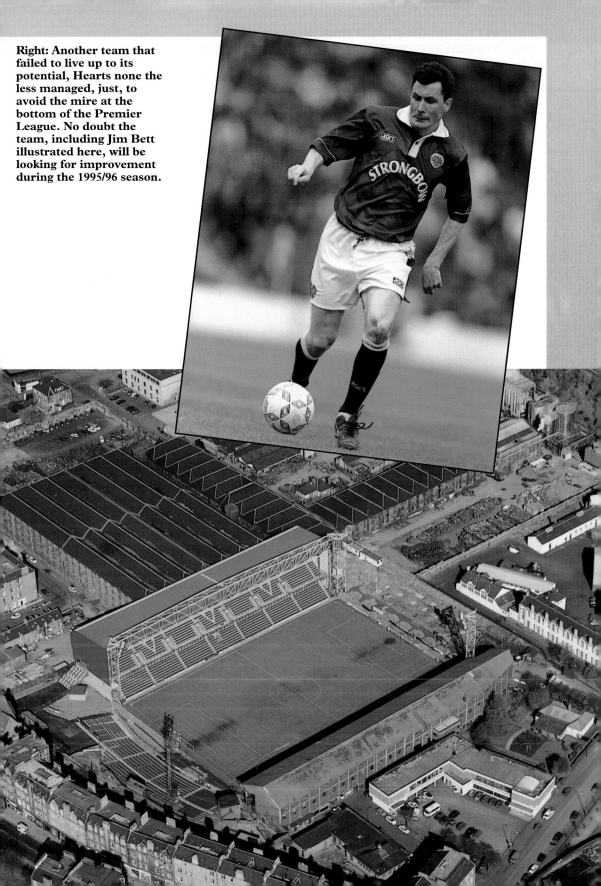

Right: Another team that failed to live up to its potential, Hearts none the less managed, just, to avoid the mire at the bottom of the Premier League. No doubt the team, including Jim Bett illustrated here, will be looking for improvement during the 1995/96 season.

RANGERS

Ibrox Stadium, 150 Edminston Drive, Glasgow, G51 3XD

Tel No: 0141 427 8500
Advance Tickets Tel No: 0141 427 8800
League: Premier Division
Brief History: Founded 1873. Founder
Members Scottish League (1890). Former
Grounds: Flesher's Haugh, moved to Burnbank
(1875), Kinning Park (1876), Ibrox Park
(1887) and Ibrox Stadium in 1899. Record
attendance 118,567.
(Total) Current Capacity: 45,407 (38,407
seated)

Club Colours: Blue Shirts, White Shorts
Nearest Railway Station: Ibrox (underground)
Parking (Coach/Bus): Albion Training Ground
Police Force and Tel No: Strathclyde 0141 445
1113
Disabled Visitors' Facilities
Wheelchairs: West enclosure
Blind: West enclosure
Anticipated Development(s): (Editor's note:
Update information regarding Ground not
advised.)

KEY
C Club Offices
S Club Shop
E Entrance(s) for visiting
supporters

❶ Edminston Drive
❷ Ibrox (Underground station)
❸ Copland Road
❹ Govan Stand
❺ M8 Motorway
❻ Broomloan Stand
❼ To Glasgow Central BR
station

Left: Rangers' much-travelled ex-England striker Mark Hateley will be joined in the Scottish champion's line up for the 1995/96 season by a current England star — Paul Gascoigne, who has been recruited from the Italian team Lazio.

AIRDRIEONIANS

**Broomfield Park,
Gartlea Road,
Airdrie, ML6 9JL**

League: Division 1
(Groundsharing with
Clyde F.C. 1994/95 season
until construction of new
ground)

ALBION ROVERS

**Cliftonhill Stadium,
Main Street,
Coatbridge,
Strathclyde,
ML5 3RB**

League: Division 3
(Will groundshare with
Aidrie eventually when new
Airdrieonians ground
completed)

ALLOA ATHLETIC

**Recreation Park,
Clackmannan Rd,
Alloa, FK10 1RR**

League: Division 3

ARBROATH

**Gayfield Park,
Arbroath,
DD11 1QB**

League: Division 3

AYR UNITED

**Somerset Park,
Tryfield Place,
Ayr, KA8 9NB**

League: Division 2

BERWICK RANGERS

**Shielfield Park,
Shielfield Terrace,
Tweedmouth,
Berwick upon
Tweed, TD15 2EF**

League: Division 2

BRECHIN CITY

**Glebe Park,
Trinity Road,
Brechin, Angus,
DD9 6BJ**

League: Division 3

CALEDONIAN THISTLE

**Kingsmills Park,
Kingsmills Road,
Inverness**

League: Division 3
(Amalgamation of 'Inverness
Caledonian' and 'Inverness
Thistle' and elected to
Scottish League 1994/95
season)

CLYDE

**Broadwood
Stadium,
Cumbernauld,
Strathclyde**

League: Division 2

CLYDEBANK

**Kilbowie Park,
Arran Place,
Clydebank,
G81 2PB**

League: Division 1

COWDENBEATH

**Central Park,
High Street,
Cowdenbeath,
KY4 9EY**

League: Division 3

DUMBARTON

**Boghead Park,
Miller Street,
Dumbarton,
G82 2JA**

League: Division 1

DUNDEE

**Dens Park
Stadium,
Dens Road,
Dundee, DD3 7JY**

League: Division 1

DUNFERMLINE ATHLETIC

**East End Park,
Halbeath Road,
Dunfermline, Fife**

League: Division 1

EAST FIFE

**Bayview Park,
Wellesley Road,
Methil, Fifeshire,
KY8 3AG**

League: Division 2

EAST STIRLINGSHIRE

**Firs Park,
Firs Street,
Falkirk, FK2 7AY**

League: Division 3

FALKIRK

**Brockville Park,
Hope Street,
Falkirk, FK1 5AX**

League: Premier Division

FORFAR ATHLETIC

**Station Park,
Carseview Road,
Forfar, Tayside**

League: Division 2

GREENOCK MORTON

**Cappielow Park,
Sinclair Street,
Greenock,
PA15 2TY**

League: Division 1

HAMILTON ACADEMICAL

**Douglas Park,
Douglas Park Lane,
Hamilton,
ML3 0DF**

League: Division 1
(Expecting to groundshare
with Partick Thistle for
1995/96 season until
construction of new ground).
Partick Thistle's ground is
illustrated here.

HIBERNIAN

**Easter Road
Stadium,
Albion Road,
Edinburgh,
EH7 5PG**

League: Premier Division

KILMARNOCK

**Rugby Park,
Rugby Road,
Kilmarnock,
Ayrshire, KA1 2DP**

League: Premier Division

LIVINGSTON

**Meadowbank
Stadium,
London Road,
Edinburgh,
EH7 65AE**

League: Division 2
Meadowbank Thistle changed
its name to Livingston for the
start of the 1995/96 season.
The club will continue to play
at Meadowbank Stadium until
late 1995, when it will move to
a new ground at Almondvale
Park, Livingston, Lothian.

MONTROSE

**Links Park Stadium,
Wellington Street,
Montrose,
DD10 8QD**

League: Division 2

MOTHERWELL

**Fir Park,
Fir Park Street,
Motherwell,
ML1 2QN**

League: Premier Division

PARTICK THISTLE

**Firhill Park,
90, Firhill Road,
Glasgow, G20 7AL**

League: Premier Division

QUEEN OF THE SOUTH

**Palmerston Park,
Terregles Street,
Dumfries**

League: Division 2

QUEENS PARK

**Hampden Park,
Mount Florida,
Glasgow, G42 9BA**

League: Division 3
(NB * Play at Hampden Park,
therefore covered in detail on
pp 192-193)

RAITH ROVERS

**Stark's Park,
Pratt Street,
Kirkcaldy, KY1 1SA**

League: Premier Division

ROSS COUNTY

**Victoria Park,
Dingwall,
Ross-shire,
IV15 9QW**

League: Division 3

ST JOHNSTONE

**McDiarmid Park,
Crieff Road,
Perth, PH1 2SJ**

League: Division 1

ST MIRREN

**St Mirren Park,
Love Street,
Paisley, PA3 2EJ**

League: Division 1

STENHOUSEMUIR

**Ochilview Park,
Gladstone Road,
Stenhousemuir,
FK5 5QL**

League: Division 2

STIRLNG ALBION

**Forth Bank Stadium,
Spring Terse,
Stirling, FK7 7UJ**

League: Division 2

STRANRAER

**Stair Park,
London Road,
Stranraer,
DG9 8BS**

League: Division 2

Notes

Notes

 Aerofilms

Aerofilms was founded in 1919 and has specialised in the acquisition of aerial photography within the United Kingdom throughout its history. The company has a record of being innovative in the uses and applications of aerial photography.

Photographs looking at the environment in perspective are called oblique aerial photographs. These are taken with Hasselblad cameras by professional photographers experienced in the difficult conditions encountered in aerial work.

Photographs looking straight down at the landscape are termed vertical aerial photographs. These photographs are obtained using Leica survey cameras, the products from which are normally used in the making of maps.

Aerofilms has a unique library of oblique and vertical photographs in excess of one and a half million in number covering the United Kingdom. This library of photographs dates from 1919 to the present and is continually being updated.

Oblique and vertical photography can be taken to customers' specification by Aerofilms' professional photographers.

To discover more of the wealth of past or present photographs held in the library at Aerofilms or to commission new aerial photography to your requirements, please contact:

Hunting Aerofilms Limited
Gate Studios
Station Road
Borehamwood
Herts WD6 1EJ

Telephone 0181-207-0666
Fax 0181-207-5433